Capitalism and the
Construction of Old Age

Critical Texts in Social Work and the
Welfare State

General Editor: Peter Leonard

Published

Forthcoming

Capitalism and the
Construction of Old Age

Chris Phillipson

M

First published 1982 by
THE MACMILLAN PRESS LTD
London and Basingstoke
Companies and representatives
throughout the world

ISBN 0 333 28642 1 (hard cover)
ISBN 0 333 28644 8 (paper cover)

Typeset in Great Britain by
STYLESET LIMITED
Salisbury, Wiltshire

Printed in Hong Kong

To Jane

Acknowledgement

The author and publishers are grateful to the Editor of *The Lancet* for granting permission to quote from an editorial published 3 November 1973.

Contents

Acknowledgements

There are a number of individuals and organisations who have given support and encouragement to the completion of this book. First and foremost, Jane Taylor has been of enormous help in improving the quality of the text and providing criticism of early drafts. She has shared the experience of writing this study, becoming closely involved in many of the ideas and arguments which are developed. I owe her a considerable debt.

A number of people have offered friendship and advice during various stages of the book's completion. I would like to make particular mention of Mike and Jill Holbrook, Brian Williams, Chris Jones, Tony Novack, Aleda Erskine, and Gavin and Gill Williams. Dave Cox and Peter Tetley at Birmingham Polytechnic and Philip Abrams, Huw Beynon and Bob Roshier at Durham University have also offered me valuable help. Bob Roshier was my Ph.D. supervisor and I owe him a special debt of gratitude for his support and advice. Many of the ideas developed for my Ph.D. thesis are contained in this book and I am grateful to the SSRC for their financial support during my period of full-time study.

The inter-library loans desks at Durham and Keele, and the librarian at the Centre for Policy on Ageing, have offered valuable help and advice. Peter Leonard, and Steven Kennedy of Macmillan, have given skilled guidance at all stages of the book's development. Finally, Marion Rhodes typed my manuscript with great skill and patience and she responded quickly and with great forebearance to numerous deadlines.

University of Keele
December 1981   CHRIS PHILLIPSON

Editor's Introduction

The fact that in capitalist society people are valued primarily in economic terms is nowhere more clearly demonstrated than by an examination of social policy towards the elderly. In recent years the term 'ageism' has been invented to identify a wide range of social practices which discriminate against people on account of their old age, from institutional policies and activities which abuse and harm the elderly to typically 'ageist' remarks which dismiss, belittle and insult them. The study of ageism as a social phenomenon in a wide range of societies is an important development which deserves widespread support on the Left. It is necessary, however, for such studies to be firmly located structurally so that individual practices and experiences can be understood in relation to wider economic and ideological forces. In *Capitalism and the Construction of Old Age* Chris Phillipson undertakes this precise task and so makes an important contribution to the study of ageism in the welfare state as well as extend, in very significant ways, the general Marxist analysis of social policy to which this series of Critical Texts in Social Work and the Welfare State is committed.

Although we can identify elements of oppression and discrimination against the elderly in many contemporary and past societies, when we consider our own society we must first be able to identify precisely the social relations and the accompanying ideologies which support and legitimate such oppression and discrimination. So far as social policy in relation to the elderly is concerned, we can see at once that what is significant is that people generally are evaluated in relation to their accumulation of capital, their current labour power (if the market requires it) or their ability to reproduce labour power, and that therefore those without wealth who are outside both production and reproduction (the elderly and the severely handicapped) are most likely to fare badly so far far as welfare provision is concerned. Thus the treatment of the elderly is mediated by the facts of class and gender; in particular, wealthy, ruling-class elderly are highly favoured and often retain substantial power over other people's lives as well as their own, in marked contrast to the working-class elderly, especially women.

But being dismissed as of no account or being actively discriminated against is not an experience of the working-class elderly for which the Right is solely to blame. On the Left, too, patronising and dismissive attitudes and practices have been quite evident. It would be comforting to excuse such aberrations as simply reflecting elements of dominant ideology from which socialists have not yet struggled free; it must be admitted, however, that both the economism of earlier Marxist theory and practice and the emphasis on social reproduction which is more characteristic of present-day socialist feminism have at times the effect of *marginalising* the elderly. Emphasis on the revolutionary potential of, first, producers (male industrial proletarians), and then reproducers (women engaged in the task of family socialisation) has inevitably reinforced the position of the elderly as largely *redundant* as agents of radical change.

So far as the state is concerned, ideological justification for the discrimination and neglect of the working-class elderly is a tricky matter. The stigma which attaches to the elderly poor is not as public as that which, for example, attaches to black youths or single-parent mothers, and so it cannot be used so easily to fragment the working class and thus obtain support for policies directed against the elderly. The elderly poor are 'deserving' so they can be patronised, neglected, but not openly attacked. But there is a range of justifications available to support our responses to old age and these deserve very close examination. Perhaps the most important of these ideological supports is *biological reductionism*, whereby the real physiological and biological changes which take place with ageing are often utilised as a justification for denying old people the right to participate in decisions which affect them and generally to control their own lives. To emphasise, as Chris Phillipson does, the *social construction* of ageing is not to deny the facts of physical ageing, but to point to the difficulty of deciding precisely where the boundary lies and to note the way in which the latter is used to justify the former. *Psychological explanations*, of every level of sophistication and simplicity, are similarly available to account for the way the elderly poor are treated. Thus the necessary material and physical dependency of many elderly people is interpreted as 'child-like' and used to justify treating them as if they *were* children. Furthermore, infantilising the elderly eventually produces its own predicted result — old people may be induced to accept a 'child-like' role as the only legitimate way in our society of being physically dependent upon another person.

Certain *social justifications* are also available to support, in effect, policies of neglect and discrimination directed to the elderly. It is suggested, for example, that old people want to disconnect themselves from the world, to retreat from life in preparation for death. In so far as some old people wish to 'disengage' (and there is much dispute about this) we must ask ourselves to what extent this is a socially constructed disengagement from a set of social relations experienced predominantly as stigmatising and neglectful. Certainly, we must be aware of the extent to which 'disengagement theory' and other explanations of the social phenomenon of ageing are used to suggest that the elderly have only limited, simple and even subsistence needs (especially if they are very elderly working-class women) and that therefore only minimum welfare provision is necessary.

Capitalism and the Construction of Old Age shows us how minimum much of this welfare provision is. From an analysis of the major structural elements in the social construction of ageing we are able to see the very concept of 'retirement' in a clear historical context. Phillipson demonstrates, with great sensitivity coupled with an ability to draw on telling empirical material, how old age is experienced among the working class in particular and how that experience differs as between women and men. The ideological construction of old age is seen as directly reflected in a range of welfare policies and

practices, including the ways in which the elderly are responded to by doctors and social workers. But Phillipson does not
fall into the trap of fatalism in the face of the massive forces
which are ranged against the elderly poor: on the contrary,
this is a combative book which goes on to show that the
elderly have a collective role in the struggle for their own
liberation from neglect, stigma and oppression. It is a struggle
to which the Left should give sustained support.

University of Warwick
December 1981   PETER LEONARD

1
Introduction: Capitalism and the Elderly

This book has been written in a period of crisis for elderly people. Health and social services are being substantially reduced; questions are being raised about the ability of society fully to protect pensioners against price increases; older workers are urged to retire as soon as possible as a means of reducing high unemployment amongst young people. At the same time, a tremendous expansion is taking place in the number of people aged 60 and over, a development which will require significant increases in resources to the welfare state, if health and living standards are to be maintained. The broad dimensions of these demographic changes are well understood, and are not the object of detailed scrutiny in this book. Instead, it aims first to develop a critical account of the position of elderly people in a capitalist society, and second to analyse the responses of the state to the emergence of retirement.

In placing the emphasis on the elderly and capitalist social relations this study is less concerned with old age as a biological and pychological problem. We are rather more interested in old age as a problem for a society characterised by major inequalities in the distribution of power, income and property. Westergaard and Resler have written that:

> Subsistence poverty is indeed common among old people, the sick, the handicapped, and so on; but only because the majority of the old, sick and handicapped have previously been dependent on jobs that provided them with few or no other resources to fall back on than meagre benefits from

public funds. Rank-and-file wage earners — manual and routine non-manual — live with the risk of poverty over their heads. They face a likely prospect of poverty on retirement. And they face a threat of poverty even before that: on redundancy and if forced to work short-time; on transfer to low-paid work in the later years of working life; in sickness, in widowhood, and through loss of subsidiary household earnings. The risk of poverty at two stages of the working-class life cycle — in childhood and the child-rearing phase of working life — has been markedly reduced during this century: this for the simple reason that families are now much smaller than they were, and child-bearing is compressed within a short span of years. But poverty in old age is more common than it was, because more workers live on to experience it. To the bourgeoisie, by contrast, the risk of subsistence poverty is remote. High earnings, fringe benefits, greater job security, the incremental rise of the typical life cycle, the consequent relative ease of individual 'planning' and saving — all these confer relative immunity. And property ownership gives total immunity.

                    (Westergaard and Resler, 1975, pp. 124–5)

Hitherto, class and gender relations have been given inadequate treatment in studies on the elderly. Despite the development of more radical approaches by French and North American researchers (see, for example, Guillemard, 1977; Marshall, 1981; Myles, 1981), British research has only recently begun to explore the interaction between social and economic inequalities and experiences in later life (the work of Peter Townsend is an obvious exception). I would argue that undue weight has been given to biological and psychological changes in old age (and the deterioration seen to accompany them), in contrast to the role played by the economic and political environment.

The neglect of issues associated with a political economy of old age has had some important repurcussions. In most commentaries on the elderly, it has usually been assumed that the types of problem associated with old age can easily be resolved within the framework of a capitalist society.

Research on the elderly invariably comes to the conclusion that with more government aid, additional family support and voluntary help, adequate services will emerge. This book will question that viewpoint. There is little evidence that, given an expanding economy, capitalism would contribute the massive resources which elderly people require (the historical picture to emerge in Chapters 3 and 6 supports this view). Moreover, when capitalism is in crisis, the speed with which resources are removed, both from the elderly and from other groups, indicates the tenuous hold of any legislation which is conceded. Yet this book will maintain that, regardless of the state of the economy at particular periods, *the logic of capitalism as a productive and social system is irreconcilable with meeting the needs of elderly people.* We can see this in four very obvious ways:

(1) Whenever capitalism is in crisis — as in the 1930s or in the early 1980s — it is inevitably working-class people (particularly those who become unemployed and/or are forced into retirement) who suffer most. Indeed, what we see is an attempt by capitalism to solve its problems through cuts in the living standards of working people. The expansion in, for example, the number of people entering early retirement is a thinly disguised attempt to reduce the social impact of unemployment. Many of those who retire early, once their 'golden handshakes' have been exhausted, experience many years of poverty, with no chance of re-entering the labour market, except in the most menial of jobs. Certainly, in terms of the sacrifices which are constantly being urged upon working people, the price can be very high.

(2) Capitalism has a distinct set of priorities which almost always relegates social and individual needs behind the search for profits and the maintenance of defence and of law and order. In a 1979 interview in the magazine *Social Work Today*, Patrick Jenkin (then Secretary of State for Social Services) was asked: 'You would put defence spending as a higher priority above the elderly, the infirm and other disadvantaged?'

JENKIN: Of course. If we did not defend ourselves with the three per cent growth target which is the NATO target to which we are committed, then whether it is the elderly, the mentally handicapped or the ill or Uncle Tom Cobley and all, our lives would be at great peril.

SWT: You personally believe in that?

JENKIN: Yes, of course I do.

(Social Work Today, October 1979)

In line with this philosophy, while social services have been cut back, defence spending has increased as a percentage of Gross Domestic Product (GDP). The £7,500 million programme on Trident missiles is the clearest illustration of this trend.

(3) Capitalism as a social system can have a disastrous impact on the lives of elderly people. Through the decline of major industries, areas which were once prosperous fall into decay, creating sub-standard housing, loss of jobs and the migration of younger workers with families (Community Development Project, 1977). Elderly people find themselves caught in a 'scissors' between their own need for better services, and the steady decline of facilities within their neighbourhood (a decline being accelerated by the early 1980s' expenditure cuts).

(4) Capitalism remains a system of exploitation: a ruling class still appropriates and controls the wealth produced by the working class. For Marx:

The free labourer. . . sells himself and, indeed, sells himself piecemeal. . . the worker belongs neither to an owner nor to the land, but 8, 10, 12, 15 hours of his daily life belong to him who buys them. The worker leaves the capitalist to whom he hires himself whenever he likes and the capitalist discharges him whenever he thinks fit, as soon as he no longer gets any profit out of him, or not the anticipated profit. But the worker, whose sole source of livelihood is the sale of his labour power, cannot leave the whole class of purchasers, that is the capitalist class, without renouncing his existence.

(Cited in Blackburn, 1976, p. 17)

When the older worker steps permanently outside the wage

system he or she becomes reliant on personal savings, an occupational pension or the state pension. In fact, most older people (over 70 per cent) rely on the state pension as their main source of income. Yet, at the present time this pension (for a married couple) is equivalent to just 50 per cent of the average take-home pay of an industrial worker. For those without significant additions to their income, the most devastating experiences can follow:

> Lack of finance for other things means lack of choice in housing (and the elderly certainly figure largely amongst those in poor housing), in consumer goods, in recreational and other facilities. The value of increased free time in retirement is restricted when, at the same time, income is diminished. All this too at a time when the need for expensive items has perhaps never been greater — a washing machine to help arthritic hands, a refrigerator to save daily trips to the shops on shaky legs. And how does it feel to be in this position? In a survey of elderly workers many revealed that it had been the feelings of poverty that had been the hardest thing to bear about retirement, the inability to participate in social life as a normal member of society, simply to be able to ask people to 'Have a drink'. Current trends towards early retirement will mean for many a very long time in this disadvantaged position — even with retirement at 65 this period can exceed 30 years.
> (Trade Union Studies Information Unit, 1979, p. 14).

RADICAL PERSPECTIVES ON OLD AGE

A final aim of this study is to provide radical perspectives on old age for workers in the health and social services. The ageing of the population has enormous implications for this group. Yet there have been few attempts either to develop a critical analysis of work with the elderly or the outline of alternatives. The development of a radical approach is beginning to emerge in this country: the work of Walker (1980 and 1981) on the political economy of old age, Minns (1980) on occupational pensions, Means (1981) on the development of domiciliary services — these are just a few examples of a more critical approach to questions of ageing. There have also been important contributions from trade unions such as COHSE (e.g. *In Defence of the Old*, 1981). These developments are of considerable importance and the work of such writers and organisations has been of immense help in shaping the ideas and perspectives developed in this book.

THE PLAN OF THE BOOK

This book falls into three sections. In Chapters 2 and 3 we examine the construction of old age, both historically and in terms of contemporary economic and social policies. Chapters 4 and 5 utilise a Marxist approach to class and gender relations to analyse individual experiences of ageing and retirement. In Chapters 6 to 9 we examine a number of themes in relation to ageing and the welfare state. Chapter 6 considers postwar social policy and the elderly, Chapter 7 the elderly and the health and social services, Chapter 8 reviews the politics of ageing, and in Chapter 9 we draw together elements for a political economy of retirement and old age.

2
The Social Context of Ageing and Retirement

That we live in an ageing society, with increasing numbers both of the wholly retired and the very elderly, can hardly have escaped the attention of anyone connected with the welfare state. The advent of such a society has, in the main, been greeted with considerable alarm. We hear of fears about the impact of an 'age explosion', and pessimism about the economic and social burden of large numbers of elderly people. The elderly have now achieved the status of a social problem, with their appearance in textbooks on deviancy and social control indicating a weakening in traditional preoccupations with youth.

This situation reflects two elements in the social context of ageing: first, as a society we are still in the early stages of interpreting and understanding old age; second, old age is still identified as a period of social redundancy, with the 'non-productiveness' of the old being a pervasive theme in the history of social policy.

In this chapter I shall present an outline of the social and economic context behind the process of ageing and retirement. For a more detailed review of this area numerous publications are now available. The work of the Age Concern Research Unit (see, in particular, *Profiles of the Elderly*, vols 1–6) is of considerable importance; and surveys from the Office of Population Censuses and Surveys (see, for example, Hunt, 1978; Parker, 1980) have provided useful data. Publications such as *Social Trends*, the *General Household Survey* and the *Family Expenditure Survey* should also be referred to for information on the elderly. A number of textbooks are now available reviewing basic issues behind the rise of an ageing population (Bosanquet, 1978; Carver and Liddiard, 1978; Gray and Wilcock, 1981; Tinker, 1981). Recent cross-cultural data on the elderly can be found in Palmore (1980) and Hobman (1978). A summary of this information is presented below, in preparation for a more detailed analysis in succeeding chapters.

THE DEMOGRAPHIC CONTEXT

The number of elderly people (i.e. women over 60 and men over 65) has increased this century from 2.9 million in 1911 to 9.8 million in 1981.[1] As a percentage of the United Kingdom's population this has meant an increase from 6.8 per cent in 1911 to 17.7 per cent in 1981. However, it is important to note two contrasting demographic movements. Thus between 1978 and 2011 the number of people aged 65—74 is expected to fall by 13 per cent, largely because of casualties in the Second World War and postwar emigration. On the other hnd, in the same period, the number of people aged 75 plus is likely to increase by 24 per cent; by the end of the century the very old, of whom two-thirds will be women, will constitute 45 per cent of all elderly people (Abrams, 1979).

The above trends reflect both the long-term decline in the birth rate and the effect of more people surviving into old age (primarily because of the decline in infant mortality). While, in a pre-industrial society, the death of young children (at rates of 50 per cent or more) produced a disbelief in ageing, in our society human longevity is increasingly taken for granted. In 1931 there were fewer than 10 people over the normal retirement age for every 100 under the age of 15; forty years on this had increased to 70 elderly to every 100 young people (Davis, 1976).

In the twentieth century, then, the aged have become more visible. We should not be surprised or dismayed at this prospect. The high death rates of children and younger workers both in feudal society and in the early history of capitalism reflect the enormous inequalities in those societies. That such inequalities continue to exist is reflected in class differences in chances of survival into retirement. If you are in social class 5, for example, you are 2½ times more likely to die before you retire than if you are in social class 1 (Counter Information Services, 1980; see also Townsend, 1979). Differences in mortality, however, are only one indicator of the continuing influence of class relations in determining the quality of life in retirement. For the wage-earner, in fact, the fear of poverty in old age still remains dominant, the advent of mass unemployment and earlier retirement aggravating fears of financial insecurity.

THE FINANCIAL CONTEXT

The association of retirement and old age with financial impoverishment is a common one and an important contributory factor to the low expectations held about retirement. Historically, social attitudes to the aged have been extremely ambivalent, with periods of famine constantly exposing the elderly's position as one of being 'an unproductive element' in societies dependent on human labour power (Hufton, 1974). Country labourers feared old age as a time when they would be evicted from their cottages because they were too old to work (Gaudie, 1974). Poverty in the village might lead to the withdrawal of help previously given by relatives and friends (Anderson, 1971); and with inadequate savings and no alternative accommodation, the labourer would ultimately be driven to the workhouse. For the industrial worker, the picture, until the introduction of pensions, was little different. Most older workers would have to depend on their families for financial support – a dependence which, given recurring trade and economic crises, could often be burdensome. Most, as Stearns (1975) notes, laboured until they dropped.

Today the majority of the elderly are wholly retired, and the threat of the workhouse has been removed. Yet some enduring features in their economic and social position remain, particularly their relative poverty compared with other age groups. It is calculated that around 2 million old people live at or below the poverty line. Nearly 20 per cent of pensioners get supplementary benefits and the Department of Health and Social Security estimates that a further 900,000 pensioners are eligible but do not claim. Very few of the elderly have significant amounts of savings or assets. In 1977 most claimants for supplementary pensions had no capital at all and few had more than £1,249, the amount that was at that time disregarded in calculating weekly benefit (Tinker, 1981; see also Hunt, 1978; Townsend, 1979).

The low income of elderly people means that a large percentage of their expenditure goes on basic necessities. Among single women pensioners, expenditure on food, housing and fuel takes 63.4 per cent of their income. An elderly married couple will spend over 53.4 per cent of their income on these necessities (the comparable figure for all households is 43.5 per cent).[3]

This general picture of the material situation of the elderly should be balanced by a note on the importance of differences within the population — between younger and older pensioners, between the working-class and middle-class elderly, and between men and women. The younger retired are much more likely to have occupational pensions and to have income from work. The older pensioner is rather more likely to be entirely dependent on state benefits and much less likely to have other sources of income (Bosanquet, 1978).

Class position will be an additional influence on the amount of income received in retirement. Those formerly engaged in non-manual occupations are much more likely to recieve an occupational pension than are retired manual workers. Class differences are also pronounced in the amount of occupational pension received. Layard *et al.* (1978), in work for the Royal Commission on the Distribution of Income and Wealth, found that the average occupational pension for those from professional and managerial occupations was £20 per week, compared with £5 per week for those from unskilled manual occupations. Such differences reflect major inequalities between the working-class and middle-class retired. While many white-collar groups have won the right to retirement at 60, together with an occupational pension, such rights have been gained by only a limited number of manual workers. Yet the latter face a substantial drop in their earnings in later life, as well as greater vulnerability to unemployment and redundancy (Showler and Sinfield, 1981). These material differences, combined with the poorer health and lower life expectancy of manual workers, may cause considerable stress in the transition to retirement; pessimism about the future may also make workers disinclined to prepare for their future retirement.

Inequalities of class interact with those of sex to produce a further strand of differention in old age. Two-thirds of pensioners are women, and while a married couple are more likely to live above the poverty line, the greater life expectancy of women means that with the death of her husband the woman finds herself falling back on to, or below, the poverty line: 48 per cent of all widows live at or below supplementary benefit level. For the single woman, low income at work, plus discrimination in respect of access to occupational pension schemes, combine to produce almost total reliance on the state retirement pension. In this context, Hewitt has summarised the main divisions in old age as follows:

> Single pensioners are more likely to be poor than are married couples; the very old are far more likely to be poor than the recently retired. Women – particularly the very elderly, single, or widowed woman – are most likely to be poor. Indeed poverty in this country is for the most part the poverty of women.
>
> (Hewitt, 1974, p. 12)

THE HEALTH CONTEXT

A common view of old age is to see health problems as over-riding economic and social constraints.[4] Individually, we see the elderly trapped within an inevitable deterioration of their physical and mental powers; socially, we view them as a burden, consuming disproportionate amounts of health service care. This stereotype deserves some correction and modification. The physical and mental changes accompanying old age are certainly considerable (particularly for the very elderly), and older people are indeed heavy consumers of the health services (35 per cent of health and personal social services expenditure is devoted to people 65 and over, and 20 per cent to the over 75s). But in Hunt's (1978) survey nine-tenths of the people aged 65—74 who were interviewed were able to go out on their own without assistance, nearly half had no disability which limited their activities even to a minor extent and eight out of ten asserted that their general health was good. For those aged 75—84 she found a moderate decline in mobility, health and ability to perform domestic and personal tasks, with an acceleration in these trends for those 85 and over.

Differences between the young elderly (65—74) and the very elderly (75-plus) thus complicate the health picture. In addition, we need to recognise the extent to which social factors may contribute to the poor health of many elderly people. Two examples may be used in illustration.

First, environmental factors such as poverty, bereavement and reduced social status may themselves precipitate mental health problems. Palmore, for example, has suggested that:

there is considerable evidence that the multiple stress associated with old age, such as loss of income, loss of social role, bereavement, isolation, and loss of cognitive functioning, often combine to produce the higher rates of severe mental illness found among the aged in our society.

(Palmore, 1973, p. 48)

These stresses are often ignored by those involved with the elderly. As MIND points out: 'We tend, wrongly, to see the problems of elderly people as unavoidable and insoluble, as being part of "growing old". And elderly people to some extent share in the. . . low expectations [held by] society' (1979, p.19).

Second, there are important differences in health status within the elderly population. An Age Concern survey suggested that 35 per cent of people in the more favoured social group (AB) were very fit compared with 19 per cent among those who had been doing unskilled or semi-skilled manual work (CE); 9 per cent of those who had been professionals or managers were in the highest incapacity group compared with 22 per cent of people who had been doing semi-skilled or un-skilled work (Bosanquet, 1978, p. 24). As Bonsanquet re-marks; 'good health and affluence go together, and differences in fortune which exist throughout the life span are still there in striking form in old age' (1978, p. 24).

Household composition is a further source of differentia-tion. In Abrams's (1978) survey of men and women aged 75 or over who lived alone, 21 per cent of the former and 19 per cent of the latter claimed to experience long spells of depression (the comparable figures for those living with others were 5 per cent for men, and 12 per cent for women).

THE POLITICS OF OCCUPATIONAL PENSIONS

One of the most striking developments since the Second World War has been the growth of occupational pensions. In 1936 only about 2½ million employees were in occupational pension schemes. After the war the number increased rapidly to between 6 and 7 million, and it increased by a similar amount again by the mid-1960s. This development has gener-ated a striking disparity in the political economy of old age. On the one hand, there is the poverty and hardship experi-enced by millions of pensioners; on the other hand, there is the increasing power of the pension funds, 'enmeshed in the middle of a web of interlocking City institutions' (Maggie Brown, *The Guardian*, 19 October 1981).

The economic power of the pension funds is in striking contrast to the position of their members. Amongst the 85,000 schemes in the United Kingdom, the involvement of members in the organisation and administration of funds is highly restricted (Pelly and Wise, 1980; Government Actuary, 1981). Beynon and Wainwright's description of events at Vickers when the company introduced a new pension scheme is probably not atypical:

At Vickers this involved discussion with certain national officials of the unions, the setting up of the pension scheme (with agreed contributions and benefits) and the selection of trade union trustees for the pension fund. All this was carried out in London. There was no discussion with the workers in the plants and no member of the AUEW (the majority union representing manual workers in the company) was selected as a trustee. The matter was signed and sealed as a *fait accompli*.

(Beynon and Wainwright, 1979, p. 148)

Research by Richard Minns (1980) has analysed the day-to-day control by financial institutions of pension funds. His research showed the extent to which banks derived voting power from this control and that pension fund money could be used both to support other banking activities and provide other additional income for financial institutions. Finally, the concentration of power which pension funds represent can have important political repercussions:

The increasing size of the funds, the concentration of their decision making — work for the Wilson committee showed that 34 funds controlled 60 per cent of total fund assets — and their combined muscle with the insurance companies puts them in a position to dictate terms to the government. During 1976 and 1978 the Labour government faced at least three such investment strikes. By insisting on higher interest rates before buying gilts the institutions forced their own credit squeeze on the economy. It is a source of irony for the worker as capitalist in his pension fund, that by protecting his pension, he may be squeezing himself out of a job.

(Dumbleton and Shutt, 1979, p. 337)

The increasing power of pension funds raises some important issues. For example, can their financial resources be used in the area of social and economic welfare, to help to create a new industrial infrastructure in socially depressed areas, or to provide financial backing to workers' plans for socially useful products. The idea of an alternative investment strategy for pension funds has been discussed by Sue Ward (1981) and Richard Minns (1981); at a national level, however, within the labour movement and in social policy, debates are still very limited. There is still a tendency to regard as secondary those issues connected with pensions and retirement. This is particularly the case in respect of a broader view of retirement and old age.

How does the period of retirement relate to economic institutions? How has it been affected by changes in employment? What are the gender and class dimensions to growing old? These are crucial questions to answer if a political economy of retirement is to be developed. The following three chapters provide a basis for analysing the range of issues involved.

3
The Emergence of Retirement

INTRODUCTION

In the previous chapter we explored various dimensions of an ageing society, examining the range of conditions attached to the designation 'old' or 'retired'. In this chapter a further element will be introduced: namely, the gradual removal of older people from the labour market.[1] Historically, ageing and retirement are closely intertwined, the growth in the number of elderly people influencing both the development of pension systems and formal retirement ages. However, the relationship between demographic changes and those connected with work and employment are more subtle than this statement would suggest, for alterations in the supply and demand for labour exert an independent force on retirement patterns.

Manpower policies have in fact played a major role in influencing social attitudes and expectations about retirement. Viewed historically, we find the development of compulsory retirement on the one hand, and on the other attempts to circumvent the retirement age, either in terms of encouraging people to remain longer at work or to retire early. Thus, despite the emergence of a fixed retirement age, there has remained a flexible policy over when it is socially acceptable to retire.

One outcome of this process has been the emergence of older people as a reserve of labour. In periods of slump, for example, they may be drawn out of the labour market more quickly than other groups (particularly unskilled and semi-skilled older workers); in periods of labour shortage, the justification for retiring and becoming a 'non-producing consumer' may be questioned as part of a campaign to call back or retain people in the labour force.

Given this background, it is perhaps not surprising that individuals are often confused and uncertain in their attitudes towards retirement. The years attached to the onset of old age may be accompanied by feelings of guilt about entering the role of retiree. To be permanently retired still lacks the sense of legitimacy and purpose attached to the role of worker. Retirement has, however, emerged as the dominant experience for those over 60. I shall argue that despite this development, experiences and perceptions of retirement still reflect historical tensions between the 'productive' and 'non-productive': tensions which the welfare state has done little to remove.

THE EMERGENCE OF RETIREMENT: THE HISTORICAL BACKGROUND

The possibility of older people acting as a reserve of labour expresses in economic terms a historical consistency in attitudes towards the elderly. This amounts to an ambivalence regarding how far older people have a right to share and enjoy material resources without being engaged in full- or part-time work. The argument to be advanced is that in British capitalist society (and in most like societies) the growth in the number of elderly people (especially when combined with retirement) leads to dilemmas over the distribution of resources. Unlike children, the elderly will play no future role in production: they will consume with no prospect of actually producing. That they have spent the bulk of their lives creating wealth is usually ignored. In social policy terms they are viewed as an economic burden, a group for whom financial support must be strictly rationed and controlled.

It might be objected here that such a perspective is extreme and that it does little justice to the major attempts of reform in the postwar years. However, these attempts have left the elderly vulnerable to unemployment and redundancy and with living standards some twenty years behind the rest of the population.

OLD AGE AND RETIREMENT: THE INTERWAR PERIOD

Famine, mass unemployment and changes in fertility rates have all played a role — at different historical periods — in isolating older people, causing society to single them out as representing special difficulties. Old age, in fact, is often described not only as a burden but a factor causing long-term damage to the economy and society. In the 1950s the elderly were described as 'passengers',[2] threatening to pull down the standard of living enjoyed by society as a whole; they were a regressive element, dampening the 'initiative of youth' and playing a conservative role in social and political life. In this period, the elderly experienced the tension of being 'non-productive' in a society which demanded that everyone should work and be productive. By contrast, in the 1930s, it was their work role which came under attack, and their ability to withstand idleness which was applauded.

These examples illustrate the subordinate role played by elderly people in this society. Pressure for retirement and for the adoption of formal retirement ages has almost always come from without. The feelings of workers themselves are thrust aside in the attempts to meet wider economic imperatives.

Prior to the implementation and maturation of pension schemes, the fear of poverty allowed very few workers to retire voluntarily. In Britain at the turn of the century, for example, two-thirds of men over 65 were employed. Often, however, older workers (particularly in the manual sector) were forced into low-paid and unskilled work: employment which rarely provided a sufficient surplus for workers' old age. This is reflected in the huge amount of poverty affecting the elderly at the time. In Edwardian Britain, one in ten of the population aged over 65 lived in the workhouse. By the age of 70, one in five would be a pauper, and for those who reached 75, one in three would be reduced to that state (Thompson, 1975). In most of the social surveys conducted in Britain during the 1920s and 1930s, for example the *New Survey of London Life and Labour*, Rowntree's return visit to York, Herbert Tout's study of living standards in Bristol, old age was identified as one of the major sources of poverty.[3]

Stevenson's review of social conditions in the 1920s and 1930s reported that the London survey

> found that in the east end of London, as in the London area as a whole, poverty was still rife amongst the elderly. As the new survey observed, the pension for a single person was in itself insufficient to place them above the poverty line if they were living alone. The London survey found that in many cases the poverty of the elderly was associated with bad housing conditions. For many the Poor Law Institution with its stigma as the 'workhouse' was the final destination when incapacity and lack of support from relatives prevented them from continuing on their own.
>
> (Stevenson, 1977, p. 108)

In the 1930s Rowntree estimated that in York 33 per cent of old-age pensioners were living below even his own stringent poverty line, and throughout this decade the numbers of pensioners receiving supplementary relief from the Poor Law continued at well over 200,000 (7,500 in a city the size of Liverpool alone).[4] By 1931, 63.2 per cent of the population over 65 were receiving old-age pensions, with 75.5 per cent of those over 70 in receipt. However, a contemporary observer noted that 'The scale of pension is too low for voluntary retirement except in cases where other resources are available. An income of £1 a week is hardly adequate for a married couple who have no other resources, and even this amount is not received unless the wife is over pensionable age' (Owen, 1935, p. 81).

Certainly, the figure of just over 200,000 applying for poor relief massively understated the extent of poverty in old age. Many people were discouraged from applying for relief because of the detailed scrutiny they had to undergo via the Public Assistance Committees. Branson and Heinemann describe the process as follows:

> An application for poor relief meant a visit from the relieving officer who asked a great many personal questions. In many areas the applicants would then have to appear

before a relief sub-committee of the Council and answer further questions. If he was granted relief he would line up once a week to draw the money. Some of it might be issued in kind, or in relief tickets which could be exchanged for specific items at local shops. Every fourteen weeks this procedure would be gone through again.

(Branson and Heinemann, 1971, p. 23.)

Notwithstanding the rigour of this procedure, throughout the 1970s the elderly formed 'a continually large proportion of those forced to apply for public charity' (Gilbert, 1970, p. 253), though it was still a surprise to many officials when in 1940, with the introduction of the supplementary pension, the number qualifying for this pension soon topped the million mark, as opposed to the 400,000 that had been expected. A leading article in *The Times* on 19 August 1940 commented:

The proved need for supplementary pensions has been far greater than had been supposed, and when the final figures are ascertained the number of recipients will be about a million. Already with 100,000 applications still to be adjudicated, the total is only 50,000 less than a million. There has therefore been a remarkable discovery of secret need.

The Times concluded that 'The surprise of the investigation is that for so many old people the level of existence should have been so low.' In fact, by 1945, out of a total of just under 4 million old-age pensioners, the number receiving the supplementary pension was 1½ million: a low level of existence indeed! The elderly were placed in an increasingly invidious position relative to all other age groups with the onset of the depression of the 1930s. On the one hand, existing pension legislation proved manifestly inadequate to provide them 'with independence' (Gilbert, 1970, p. 253). On the other hand, the years of mass unemployment brought increased calls for the elderly to retire from remunerative employment. We know little about how this economic contradiction expressed itself in social relationships. Certainly, the insecurity of the elderly cannot have been lessened in the period from the Edwardian era through to the 1930s. Ellis Smith MP told the House of Commons in November 1938: 'Old grandfathers and grandmothers are afraid to eat too much food lest they should be taking the bread out of the mouths of their grandchildren.' Another MP told of 'an old man bent and worn, who has worked in the steel industry all his life', and who had said: 'I only have 10s 0d. a week. I am living with my son, but his wife says she can no longer afford to keep me. I don't know what to do. I don't want to go to the workhouse, but there is nothing else to be done' (cited in Branson and Heinemann, 1971, p. 229).

All this was a far cry from those Oxfordshire villagers whose 'tears of gratitude' ran down their cheeks on first receiving the old-age pension back in 1909. (Thompson, 1973). It was a far cry also from the experience of old age at the upper end of the class structure. Simone de Beauvoir (1972) has noted how the words 'old age' cover two profoundly different kinds of reality according to whether one is referring to the oppressed or the exploiting classes – a point which is as valid for Britain as elsewhere. J. B. Priestley in his *English Journey* commented upon the 'elderly gentlefolk' on the Isle of Wight, 'tucked away in charming old manor houses or converted farms... watch[ing] the decay of their incomes and keeping open houses for young male relatives on leave from the East' (1934, pp. 20–1). But decaying incomes should not be equated with grinding poverty, and whilst 'charming manor houses' may have been in short supply the numbers opting to move to seaside resorts – especially the south coast – for their retirement, accelerated in the 1930s. To take three Sussex resorts as examples, the proportion of people of pensionable age in Bexhill went up from 11.8 in 1921 to 15.0 in 1931, accelerating to 28.0 by 1951; for Hastings the figures for these years were 13.9, 18.2 and 23.9; for Worthing they were 14.4, 18.8, 29.7; the figures for England and Wales as a whole were 7.8, 9.6 and 13.8 (Karn, 1977).

Such are the ironies of the class structure. Old age, while moving some to the workhouse, moved others to the sea, leaving, though, for the majority in between the weary monotony enforced by life around the poverty line.

RETIREMENT AND THE LABOUR MOVEMENT

Despite the inadequacy of pensions, changes in production methods, combined with the depression, forced many workers into retirement. Thane (1978) suggests that the spread of pensions at all occupational levels — from the late nineteenth century onwards — is best explained by growing demands for greater efficiency and increased productivity in a variety of occupations. She argues:

> In face of foreign competition, the labour process intensi-fied to increase production in a number of occupations, such as mining, textiles and engineering. Trade Unionists complained that this led to earlier redundancy of men too old to work at the required pace. They also believed that workmen's compensation legislation, introduced in 1897, requiring employers to insure against accidents at work, made employers eager to lay-off older and possible accident-prone workers. Employers both introduced occupational pensions and pressed for a state scheme as this would let them lay off older workers with clear consciences.
>
> (Thane, 1978, p. 236)

Peter Stearns (1975), in his study of industrialisation between 1890 and 1919, reported older workers being threat-ened by the obsolesence of their skills and by work speed-up. British metal workers claimed that the latter caused prema-ture ageing, and found that many of their employers judged them 'too old at forty'. Railroad employees found that senior workers were passed over in a desire to promote younger workers, and particular anger was directed at eye tests that could result in the dismissal of older engineers (see Stearns, 1975, pp. 61–2).

The depression years increased the difficulties faced by older workers, caught as they were between the trap of inade-quate pensions and shrinking job opportunities. The contrac-tion of the old-established industries, e.g. cotton, shipbuilding, mining, had raised unemployment to crisis levels, and the search for ways of easing the situation was now to dominate political debate. In this context older workers were an immediate focus of attention. As early as 1924 Philip Snowden, Labour Chancellor of the Exchequer, had suggested that in times of unemployment the old should retire, and this theme was to be taken up at party and trade-union conferences in the following years. A report adopted by the TUC Congress in 1929 on industrial reorganisation and industrial relations suggested that

> If by some more liberal retiring allowance than the present [pension] affords, a greater inducement could be given to those above the age of 65 to take a well earned rest from their work to allow the younger men, who are waiting for a job, to come in to their place, then a step forward would be taken in both industrial efficiency and in diminishing the numbers of those who today are on the Unemployment Register.
>
> (Trades Union Congress, 1919, p. 195)

At the Transport and General Workers' Union Biennial Delegate Conference in 1929 a resolution was carried stating 'That in view of the superannuation schemes being taken up throughout the country, our parliamentary representatives be instructed to raise the question of keeping pensioners out of competitive employment' (TGWU, 1929, p. 10). The same conference also passed a resolution calling for increased pensions (one pound a week for men over 65, plus a further pound for their wives) which would enable men to retire from work, though at the same time the resolution insisted that this would be 'only a palliative and [is] not meant as a solution to unemployment' (TGWU, 1929, p. 30). A year earlier the Labour Party's annual conference also recorded support for more generous provision 'for the veterans of industry' to help reduce the number of workers competing for jobs. Skidelsky goes as far as saying that removing the old from industry was 'Labour's one distinctive cure for unemployment' (1975, p. 184), and without doubt there was considerable activity directed towards examining the feasibility of an emergency retirement plan. On 29 June 1929 the minister concerned with employment, J. H. Thomas, had appointed a sub-committee to look at the possibility of introducing retirement pensions for industrial workers. The sub-committee was composed of George Lansbury (First Commissioner of Works), Oswald Mosley (Chancellor of the Duchy of Lancaster) and Thomas Johnston (Under-Secretary of State for Scotland), plus civil servants and a government actuary. Skidelsky in his biography of Mosley describes the various plans considered as follows:

> The first plan considered by Lansbury, Mosley and Johnston was to increase old age pensions from the existing level of 10s. a week (under the 1929 Act) to 30s. a week for married couples over 65. This, it proved, would cost the exchequer £60m a year, a prohibitive amount. On 24 July, therefore, Mosley proposed a 'temporary' scheme offering pensions at 60 to those in employment in certain depressed industries, conditional upon their retirement from work. The industries suggested were coal mining, iron and steel manufacture and shipbuilding. . . On 17 September, after the summer holidays, it was decided to drop this temporary scheme as 'insuperable difficulties' of definition would arise and only a 'comparatively small number of vacancies would be likely to be created'. Instead, the committee decided to offer all insured workers (plus railwaymen) who had reached the age of sixty by a certain date a pension of £1 a week for a married man on condition that they retired from work within six months. This turned out to be the final proposal.
>
> (Skidelsky, 1975, pp. 184–5)

The sub-committee actually presented two reports. The proposal summarised by Skidelsky was the one supported by the ministers on the sub-committee. The non-ministerial members of the committee presented a report which outlined the total of four schemes which had been considered, and evaluated their respective merits. This division reflected the civil servants' lack of enthusiasm for any of the schemes. Certainly there were major difficulties of implementation. The benefit, in terms of reducing the number of unemployed (and the consequent saving on unemployment insurance), was a matter of some controversy. Mosley had predicted as many as 200,000 job vacancies being created with such a scheme, but other estimates were more conservative than these, and it clearly depended on the extent to which younger people could or would be given the opportunity to fill the vacancies created. There were questions about the cost of the scheme (£22m. in the first year) and there was also the question of equity for other pensioners who had retired on a smaller amount. There were some 80,000 workers over 65 who had retired in 1929 on 10 shillings a week under the Conservatives' Contributory Pensions Act. The civil servants complained: 'Are these persons to see their neighbours who remained a little longer in industry now pensioned off with 30 shillings a week?' (Skidelsky, 1970, p. 119).

With the retirement plan attracting further adverse comment from the Treasury, and failing to get the support of the minister concerned with employment, the Cabinet Committee decided against its implementation. Interest in such a scheme continued, however, on the part of some Labour leaders. Mosley, for example, continued to stress the moral as well as economic advantages of such a plan. Old men, he argued, who have spent most of their lives in hard work could be released to make way for the young and energetic:

A man of 60 who has worked all his life will not suffer much demoralisation through living in idleness, but a man of 20 may suffer irreparable harm. By keeping the young in idleness we destroy the human material upon which the future of reconstructed industry must be built . . . idleness may be a boon to the old, but it is a damnation to the young. By this measure we are obeying both the dictates of nature and of economics.

(Quoted in Skidelsky, 1975, pp. 185–6)

A national association was formed in 1930 to campaign for early retirement pensions. This had Mosley as one of its vice-presidents, and a past president of the National Union of Railwaymen as president. That same year Mosley was to include his emergency retirement plan in his memorandum on unemployment sent to the Prime Minister, Ramsay Mac-Donald.

Ernest Bevin was also an early advocate of providing larger pensions as an inducement to older workers to leave their jobs. He had suggested a single consolidated insurance scheme, amalgamating the unemployment and health insurance schemes together with the old-age pension fund. According to Bullock, Bevin claimed that it was 'Far better. . . to spend money on retiring older men whose efficiency was already failing than in paying unemployment benefit to younger and more active men' (Bullock, 1960, p. 403). Bevin pursued this line throughout the early part of the 1930s, and in a series of articles in the *New Clarion* in 1933 argued, among other things, for an optional pension at the age of 60 (with a retirement condition). He calculated that this, plus a state pension of £1 a week (35 shillings a week for a married couple) at the age of 65 to everyone earning up to £1,000 per annum (again with a retirement condition), plus invalidity pensions to various groups, would release 600,000 jobs for 'younger and fitter men'. Some of these proposals were to form the basis for the comprehensive pension plan which was Bevin's contribution to the Labour Party programme in 1937.

Despite undoubted support for the reasoning of Bevin, Mosley *et al.* that it was better to secure jobs for the young and energetic than for the old, many were dubious as to how far, even if the latter were pensioned off, younger workers would step into their jobs. Rhys Davis, a Labour MP writing in the *Daily Herald* in June 1930, argued: 'Let us by all means pension the old warriors of industry as we do the heroes of the battlefields, but do not deceive ourselves by thinking that pensions or payments of any kind outside wages, either for the young or old can have any substantial effect on the disease known as unemployment.'

Eventually, in 1934, Parliament did come to discuss a motion, put forward by Labour MP John Banfield, calling for optional retirement pensions at 60. It was Banfield's belief that:

Millions of pounds now spent in unemployment pay would be better spent in pensions for the aged. . . We are spending the money, in many instances, at the wrong end. . . it should be possible. . . to pension men and women at 60 and take them out of industry and to bring in the young people to do the work of the community, the work of commerce, and the work of the nation during those years when they are most fit and able to do it.

(Hansard, 1933–4, vol. 286, col. 425)

Attractive as this idea sounded, it was inevitably riddled with all the administrative difficulties which the ministerial sub-committee had come across in 1929. How, for example, was one to ensure that those retiring really did stay out of the labour market? Would the vacancies created so easily be filled by young people? How was the scheme to be financed? None of these questions was satisfactorily answered in the ensuing debate. As a result it was resolved that the administrative problems plus the potential burden of such a scheme, both on the taxpayer and on industry, militated against its possible value for easing the employment situation.

Even if the legislative proposals failed, the high rates of unemployment for older workers and the increase in the number of wholly retired indicated that many were being forced out of employment. However, as Stearns (1977) argues, in the rush to institutionalise retirement little thought was given to what older people might do with their extra years. In the case of the working class retirement was becoming a common phenomenon:

But with this, and admitting an immense variety of individual reactions, we return to the potential tragedies prepared by working class culture (and expressed widely in the labour movement). First, of course, inadequate material preparation, so that retirement was a time of immense physical hardship. But second, the lack of any active concept of what retirement should be: it represented stopping something, work, but did it represent starting or continuing anything of interest? Without pretending to fathom the fate of retirees as a whole, for even in old age, and perhaps particularly then, individual variations are immense, we can suggest that a rapidly changing behaviour pattern found no correspondence in public policy or collective activities.

(Stearns, 1977, pp. 65–6)

The absence of any legitimating ideology for retirement at a societal level, combined with pessimism within working-class culture, was to be exploited to the full in the postwar years. Once again, the connection between manpower policy and retirement was to assert itself; in this instance, however, the emphasis was on halting the trend towards retirement, urging older workers to stay in the labour force and to delay the time when they would become 'non-productive'.

THE EMERGENCE OF RETIREMENT: THE POSTWAR EXPERIENCE

The immediate postwar period saw an urgent debate on the economic and social consequences of an ageing population and a resulting increase in research activity on topics connected with old age: Rowntree's survey on the problems of old age appeared in 1947, Sheldon's *Social Medicine of Old Age* in 1948. Following these there was a prolific discussion, particularly in the medical journals, on a range of issues associated with retirement and the elderly. Subsequently, Townsend's *The Family Life of Old People* and Shenfield's *Social Policies for Old Age*, both published in 1957, provided major contributions to filling in the outline of the debate which had emerged from the early postwar period. This was a period, then, when the hitherto rather sparse amount of research work in this area was expanded, and the first major texts and reference works became available.

On the employment front, the decline in economic activity among men over 65 continued: moving from a rate of 31.1 in 1951, to 25.0 in 1961 and 19.4 in 1971. This development, however, did not take place without considerable debate.

On the surface this period provided a more favourable environment for older people, with a new scheme of social insurance and a national health service ready to provide greater support for the needs of the elderly. There was widespread feeling that the great problem of poverty among old people had been solved and that unless there was a substantial rise in the cost of living 'real poverty need no longer exist among any class of aged persons' (Rowntree, 1947, p. 99).

However, these changes were underscored by an agitated debate on the potential harm of an ageing population and an increase in the number of wholly retired individuals. For some commentators, the former raised the possibility of a near-senile gerontocracy, hampering both economic growth and the initiatives of young people. A PEP report saw the prospects for youth in an ageing society in the following way:

> It is true that youth might acquire a scarcity value. But the emphasis on social service legislation would probably be placed too exclusively on provisions for the old — indeed there are already complaints on this score. The frustration which would be felt by the young in a country where their elders could not only always out-vote them but also put an effective damper on their initiative might well drive them into mass emigration. By reducing still further the proportion of young people, this might worsen the [economic] position beyond hope of recovery.
> (Political and Economic Planning, 1948, p. 84).

As regards retirement, all commentators were agreed that its increasing acceptance by workers was undesirable, the advent of permanent retirement on improved pensions threatening the standard of living of the entire community. The Royal Commission on Population expressed great concern on this point: 'if all the old sit back on their first pensionable birthday and draw a pension with which they compete for consumer goods made by a decreasing section of the population, the standard of life of both generations will inevitably be endangered' (1949, p. 322). This perspective on the elderly emerged within the legislative context of the National Insurance Act of 1946, an Act which, for the first time, made retirement a condition for receiving old-age pensions. Here was the supreme paradox for the development of a social policy on retirement. For in the very introduction of this condition, the government launched a major ideological offensive against the idea that it was encouraging people to withdraw from work. In this, the government was following to the letter the views of Beveridge:

> Making receipt of pensions conditional on retirement is not intended to encourage or hasten retirement. On the contrary, the conditions governing pension should be such to encourage every person who can go on working after pensionable age, to go on working and to postpone the claiming of the pension . . . The right way of encouraging postponement of retirement is to make it attractive for people who can remain at work after they have reached the minimum pension age to do so; such people should be allowed, by continuing to contribute and postponing claim to pension to qualify for an addition to the basic rate which is given if pension is claimed at the minimum age. The object of encouraging continuance at work in later life will not be attained by granting pensions without a retirement conditon. If these pensions are adequate for subsistence they will obviously encourage retirement. Even inadequate unconditional pensions will encourage retirement in many cases. There are other superannuation schemes for some of which pensions can be drawn only on retirement . . . provision of universal unconditional pensions by the state will lead many people to take this with their other superannuation provision and retire.
>
> (Beveridge, 1942, p. 96)

It is the social context which provides the main clue both to the character of government legislation and to attitudes towards retirement. This was after all a postwar society in whose economy rationing and reconstruction were the dominant themes. In this environment the possibility of an ageing population was greeted with an inevitable chorus of alarm. Beveridge himself had warned in his blueprint for the welfare state that 'it is dangerous to be in any way lavish in old age' until 'adequate provision has been assured for all other vital needs, such as the prevention of disease, and the adequate nutrition of the young' (1942, p. 42). There was, as a result, a remarkable *volte-face* in policies towards older people, particularly in relation to employment. While the prewar period stressed all the disadvantages in employing old people, the early postwar period stressed all the advantages. In the 1930s emphasis had been laid on the fact that older workers had more days off through sickness, were inefficient, and were less able to adapt to new production techniques; now their reliability, their commitment and their experience were stressed. In place of the 'virtues of retirement' of the high-unemployment 1930s, the 'dangers of retirement' became the leitmotiv of the full-employment era of the 1950s. Retirement was no longer as acceptable as it had been. The theme of an 'industrious' as opposed to 'idle' old age became dominant, the workshop replacing the armchair in the elderly's new found role of assisting the nation's economic reconstruction.

Walker noted the rise in the employment of the elderly during the war and comments from employers that they were 'steady and more reliable than many young workers' (1952, p. 169), a point which was stressed by the Chief Medical Officer for London Transport at the 1952 conference of the National Old People's Welfare Council:

> The great assets which older persons possess are conscientiousness and a stabilizing and steadying effect on the younger members of their work group. Every manager and foreman knows the valuable influence which older workers exercise on the team and I do not think that their importance in this connection is sufficiently felt by the older members themselves; it should be brought home to them that they are needed — desperately needed. It is sometimes said that nowadays people lack the desire to give a fair day's work for a fair day's pay; the majority of older workers not only have this desire but they are capable, if encouraged, of inculcating it to some extent in younger workers.
> (National Old People's Welfare Council, 1952, pp. 59—60)

The Ministry of Labour and National Service circulated a Canadian film which paid 'tribute to the reliability of older workers' (Ministry of Labour, 1953), as well as producing a special pamphlet and other material on the employment of older men and women. In the USA as well at this time there was a similar (though less intense) debate about the employment potential of older workers. The Dodge Division of the Chrysler Corporation had an 'old man's department', a workshop to which older employers could be transferred to work at their own pace. An American businessman started an 'old people's store', the main peculiarity of which was not the goods that it sold but that none of the employees was under the age of 60. Breckenridge's *Effective Use of Older Workers* cited the example of a shoe factory which

> hires older women (sometimes in their seventies) for its cutting room and welt room, for cementing and lining, for work on splitting machines, and as shoe brushers. The arm muscles of some older women appear to be stronger than those of younger women who have had their household chores reduced by vacuum cleaners and washing machines and electric irons.
>
> (Breckenridge, 1953, p. 40)

Three factors underpin this enthusiasm for employing older workers. First, there was a considerable manpower shortage in the postwar period in many parts of the country, and as the Ministry of Labour pointed out at the National Old People's Welfare Council conference referred to above 'old people are one of our few reserves of labour' (1952, p. 52). Second, there was a renewed sense of pessimism about the demographic balance between the productive and non-productive sectors of the population. Third, there were gloomy forecasts about the prospects for future economic growth. A combination of these factors increased pressure for people to delay their retirement.

From the late 1940s onwards appeals to people to stay at work started to appear in the Ministry of Labour's annual reports: appeals which became increasingly strident up to the mid-1950s. The report for 1950 emphasised the interaction between demographic changes and the economic context: 'The proportion of elderly persons among the population is increasing to such an extent that with the continuing general shortage of labour it is becoming more and more important that they should be employed wherever they are able and willing to work and their services are needed' (Ministry of Labour, 1951, p. 20).

The following year Hugh Gaitskell in his Budget speech argued that the corollary of the reduction in hours of work, the increased holidays and the later ages at which people now entered employment was that 'we should work longer and retire later'. He suggested an upward revision of the pension age. A few days later Fred Lee, Parliamentary Secretary to the Minister of Labour, made an impassioned appeal to older people thinking of retirement:

> I ask them to think again. Some of us may have become accustomed to the idea of retiring at a fixed age of 60—65, but a man of 65 can today look forward to a long period of useful life. I have no doubt that many people would have a happier and healthier old age if they *continue in their work a little longer rather than give up their routine and sink into a premature old age* [my emphasis].
>
> (*Hansard*, 1950, vol. 486, col. 849)

There was no suggestion of a happy retirement here. On the contrary, the association of retirement with premature senility became an increasing concern in this period. The possibility of withdrawal from work having potentially disastrous effects on the individual had earlier been noted by Sheldon in his pioneering work *Social Medicine of Old Age*. He wrote:

> Bearing in mind what has already been said about the importance of an adequate mental urge for the maintenance of physical health, one need have no surprise at the well-known sight of the man who retires, apparently healthy, from a profession or business to which he has devoted his life, and then dies for no particular reason in the next few years.
>
> (Sheldon, 1948, p. 193)

This argument was to be a constant theme in debates throughout the 1950s, with medical evidence being invoked to justify the economic need for workers to delay retirement. Eight years after Sheldon's work, Anderson and Cowan suggested that the medical literature was 'overwhelming in its indications that retirement is detrimental to the health of older men (1956, p. 346). Summarising the results of their own study on a group of men aged 65 and over, they argued that those men who were working were 'significantly happier' than those who retired and that to retire quite contented and mentally adjusted 'was the privilege of the few' (p. 1347). Earlier, a relationship between compulsory retirement and suicide had been suggested by Logan (1953) and by Batchelor and Napier (1953). According to the former, 'The suicide rate is high amongst elderly people. It might not be so high if more of them were given the opportunity to be useful, productive members of the community' (Logan, 1953, p. 1193).

In fact, these pessimistic judgements were premature. The literature was certainly not overwhelmed with studies of an adequate methodological and sample design to draw definite conclusions. The men in Anderson and Cowan's study, for example, were drawn from the records of those who had attended a health centre, a factor complicating any inferences which might be extended to the retired population as a whole. In Batchelor and Napier's study, which was based on forty cases of attempted suicide by people aged 60 and over, more than half of the sample had a history of mental illness, with seven having made previous suicide attempts. In addition, only eleven were actually classified as being retired, with nearly half still currently employed. Such a sample hardly constituted an adequate basis for making associations between compulsory retirement and suicide. However, despite the paucity and limitations of available data, studies and commentaries on retirement accepted as axiomatic that retirement would lead to some form of premature ageing and an early death — a point anticipated in the earlier work of Wermal and Gelbaum in a formulation which was also to become familiar: 'Medical, psychological, and sociological research indicates that, for those who are eager to work, idleness may result in serious personality disintegration' (1945, p. 16).

What was the impact of this propaganda against retirement? In the short term it undoubtedly added urgency to the drive for economic reconstruction, and labour-force participation for workers aged 55 to 64 showed a small increase. In contrast, the trend towards permanent retirement continued, as did age discrimination in hiring practices and occupational downgrading in the run-up to retirement. But the biggest impact must be measured in terms of attitudes and expectations. The sense of pessimism in working-class culture was enormously strengthened. Although it increased dramatically in its importance, retirement came to be viewed as an unnecessary evil. Moreover, apart from urging people to remain at work, few constructive proposals emerged to limit its apparently damaging effects. A few lone voices called for adequate preparation for retirement, with courses to be organised in the period leading up to retirement (e.g. Heron, 1961). In the main such pleas were ignored. Essentially they were out of step with the times, interest being centred on lengthening the period of work rather than on educating people to use retirement more constructively. Unfortunately, full employment was to be short-lived and the following decades saw a return to mass unemployment. Not only did this development confirm the permanence of retirement at 60 or 65, but the theme of early retirement became the subject of widespread debate. Just twenty years after discussion on whether the pension age should actually be raised, the talk was about retirement at 60 for men (and even earlier for some groups).

RETIREMENT IN THE 1980s AND 1990s

The position of the older worker in the labour market has changed dramatically since the early 1970s. The effects of a world economic recession, and the weakening in Britain's position *vis-à-vis* other capitalist economies, have produced high levels of unemployment. Moreover, long-term changes in technology are turning temporary slumps in employment into a permanent fixture. As a number of writers have recently argued, an important trend in the 1950s and 1960s in most capitalist countries has been the increased pace of technological innovation and the adaption of advanced labour-saving techniques. Gamble and Walton (1976) suggest that this process intensified in the 1970s with a new wave of innovation based on computers and electronics. They argue that

> Increasingly large numbers of workers are being displaced from the productive process and have to find jobs in the burgeoning service section. As Marx foresaw in *Grundrisse*, the historical tendency of capitalist accumulation is to reduce necessary labour to the minimum so as to increase surplus labour to the maximum. The rate of exploitation is raised by employing ever fewer workers, ever more machines and thus increasing productivity to its furthest extent.
>
>   (Gamble and Walton, 1976, p. 161)

This economic and technological environment was to shift once more the postion of the elderly in the labour market, and to change as well ideologies concerning retirement. The crude celebration of the work ethic, evident in much government propaganda in the early 1950s, was substantially altered. People had now to accept the need for redundancies, for 'shake-outs', and early retirement. Britain's economic position (and the condition of her industry) demanded a smaller and more efficient work-force. Given also that a high birth rate in the early 1960s was now resulting in a boom of young workers, it was the replacement of the old with the young which was to become a strong theme in government policy (e.g. the job-release scheme).

Throughout the 1970s there was an accelerated withdrawal of older workers from the labour market (Office of Population Censuses and Surveys, 1980). Moreover, older workers have continued to be disproportionately affected by redundancies, though the use of early retirement options has masked the numbers involved.

The virtual collapse of part-time work for people beyond

65 and the trend towards earlier retirement raise important issues for the labour movement. Expansion of the number of years spent in retirement has the support of many workers and trade unionists. Such a policy is seen as expanding job opportunities for younger people and giving older workers a more relaxed way of life. But some important questions must be asked: How financially secure will this life be? Will early retirement turn into yet another sacrifice by older people for the sake of giving younger people jobs? Will it simply mean reducing the number officially unemployed but expanding the number of people in poverty? If we accept a policy of job redistribution, rather than job creation, should we not argue for a new deal for the retired, whose experience in later life has often been harsh and disappointing? 'Too little to live on, too much to die on'; 'Too old to work, too young to die': such thoughts have been expressed about retirement. What will be the slogans for the future?

CONCLUDING COMMENTS

It may be argued that the inconsistencies in attitudes towards retirement reflect broader problems concerning the role of older people in industrial societies. This perspective would suggest that the elderly had a 'golden past' in which they experienced more security and support than is the case at present. Retirement, it is argued, was virtually unknown, hence there was not the problem of loss of function and status which seems so apparent today. Burgess presents this view-point in the following way:

> Family and kinship ties persist but they are no longer central and vital. The result is that the older person feels dethroned and devalued where he once reigned supreme. He can no longer count on the role of patriarch in ordering the destiny of his children and grandchildren. He cannot even be sure of being venerated and respected. In short he has lost his old role of dominance and has not yet found a new one.
>
> (Burgess, 1960, p. 272)

I do not propose to analyse here the objections to this position. Suffice to say that the work of historians such as Laslett (1977) and Thomas (1976) has effectively discredited this theme. Thomas has indicated that it is inaccurate to regard the depreciation of the elderly as a recent affair. Throughout history, he suggests, the elderly have always suffered from changes which make their experiences outmoded. In the past, if some older people did retain authority, this was more because of the resources at their disposal than any particular esteem attached to old age.

Thus the marginalisation of older people in times of rapid technological change and/or high unemployment is not peculiar to our century. We can, in fact, trace a consistent theme whereby the costs of social change are forced on to specific groups, with those such as the poor and working-class elderly being most vulnerable of all. What is peculiar to our period is the scale of marginalisation and the increase in the number of people directly involved. It is this aspect which marks a decisive and qualitative shift from previous historical epochs. The emergence of retirement and the growth in the number of people aged 60 and over is exclusive to the present century. Old age, together with retirement, has become a major stage in the life cycle, with older people themselves being recognised as a distinct social and economic category. However, this change in population and in the distribution of work has yet to find a satisfactory framework of support within society as a whole. The elderly still find themselves vulnerable to charges of being an economic burden, soaking up the resources 'derived from the exertions of others', and vulnerable also to the experiences of poverty and loneliness. The difference now is that such experiences cover millions rather than thousands of individuals, the scale of the problem ruling out the value of simple historical comparisons.

The absence of historical examples and the rapid emergence of old age as a social problem have contributed to the underdevelopment of a social policy for retirement. At an individual level, the repercussions of this have been enormous. It is to an examination of this area that we must now turn.

4

Men in Retirement and Old Age

INTRODUCTION

In this and the following chapter the large-scale changes described previously will be related more directly to individual experiences and perceptions about ageing and retirement. The focus will be on providing an account of how people approach old age, with an examination of the tensions and opportunities it brings into their lives. In developing such an account considerable problems need to be recognised by both reader and writer when evaluating certain items of information. A difficulty lies in freeing ourselves from a particular view of ageing in general and of retirement in particular: one which focuses exclusively on the redundancy of the old, and on their supposed yearning for past relationships and activities. This approach treats retirement as a personal tragedy, portraying the retired person — particularly the male — as victim of a powerful work ethic, and difficulties in adjusting to retirement are seen as reflecting a failure to find substitutes for the stimulation once provided via work.

Not surprisingly — given the economic environment — such a viewpoint was a consistent theme in publications and reports of the 1950s. Unfortunately it has remained influential despite a vastly changed economic climate and despite radically changed attitudes towards retirement. I shall argue that while this approach cannot be ignored entirely — there are without doubt important tensions in the transition to retirement — it must be modified substantially if the needs of retired people are properly to be understood. This chapter and the next present an outline of how the *individual* approaches retirement, and the impact it makes on his or her life. The focus is primarily on *men* in this chapter; the following chapter concentrates on the experience of women. Both chapters explore how variations in social class and occupation affect activities and perceptions within the retirement period.

THE ENTRY INTO RETIREMENT

The run-up to formal retirement may be marked by a number of significant changes. For many people important alterations occur in perceptions about work and work-based relationships. Among some individuals we find a subjective distancing from their occupational life – as they try out a range of interests and activities which may be taken up in greater depth in retirement. For others, objective changes (e.g. redundancy and poor health) may precipitate anxiety about the future. Conversely, we find many individuals hardly thinking at all about their retirement, delaying any decisions until the day itself.

A number of more general factors will also influence feelings in this period. For example, along with the individual's ageing, the community in which he or she lives may be ageing demographically; within the family, sons and daughters will have grown up and may have moved away. Both changes will stimulate awareness of the process of ageing and the possibility of a future period of transition.

An important question in this respect concerns the quality and quantity of resources people are able to retain in this period. Among early retirees, for example, Wedderburn (1975) has distinguished between, on the one hand, those who have lost their jobs a few years before the age of 65, who have in addition poor financial resources, and possibly a disability as well (such men enter retirement with the minimum of resources, and may find it a bitter and isolating experience, particularly if they are single); and those, on the other hand, who have chosen to retire because retirement is something to look forward to both in a positive sense (to do other things), and in a negative one (to escape from work), and who have an adequate income to support themselves in retirement. Such differences are often sharpened rather than diminished as the retirement period unfolds.

In this context, three main variations in the movement from work to retirement may be distinguished.

1. *Stable withdrawal*

Stable withdrawal involves acknowledgement of either the need for, or the likelihood of, withdrawal from full-time work, with a readiness to face up to the changes in life-style and behaviour this may engender. Accompanying this may be a feeling that the individual can no longer function as effectively at work, and that his major duties and accomplishments have been achieved. Among some groups of workers (e.g. miners) the high number who report as too ill to work in the year prior to retirement may reflect not only an objective state of health but a feeling that the individual has worked long enough and that retirement is a welcome alternative.[1]
In a recent study of voluntary early retirement, one of the most commonly mentioned factors was a belief by individuals that they 'deserved their retirement' (McGoldrick and Cooper, 1980). This applied particularly to manual workers and those already in their sixties. A study by Jacobsohn (1972) of workers in an engineering factory found that the heavier the overall job task level, the lower the 'ideal' retirement age desired by respondents.

2. *Unstable withdrawal*

Unstable withdrawal involves a situation where objective pressures such as redundancy (perhaps combined with ill-health) lead to increasing marginalisation within the labour force. In some instances unemployment and retirement may merge together as part of an extended period with declining resources.[2] The negative experiences arising from this may be reinforced by a feeling that the individual has been discarded and rejected by society. The phrase 'too old to work, too young to die' has particular relevance for people in this group.

3. *Abrupt withdrawal*

While younger people may have very positive feelings about
retirement, the evidence from some research suggests that as
retirement draws closer, people feel less favourably disposed
towards it (Lehr and Dreher, 1969). A recent survey found
that feelings about retirement varied considerably across different age groups, and that amongst those 45 and over there was
a sharp increase in anxiety (Commission of the European Communities, 1978). Such feelings may interfere with any constructive planning or preparation for retirement. A study by Crawford (1971) found that a quarter of the men and nearly half the
women interviewed had no idea at all about what to do in their
retirement. A more recent survey by Parker (1980) noted
that more than three-quarters of workers under pension age
and the early retired (just before they left work) said they
were prepared just to let things happen rather than to plan
for the future.

THE EXPERIENCE OF RETIREMENT

The formal entry into retirement may be marked by a number
of rituals and ceremonies. In a study by Crawford (1973)
four-fifths of the men interviewed had some kind of retirement ceremony, the majority occurring within working hours
and others during the lunch-break or after work altogether.
The existence of a ceremony, its timing and its participants,
are all likely to reflect class and status differences. Here are
comments from two skilled manual workers Crawford interviewed. In the first extract the ceremony was organised
during the working day, in the second after work had finished:

> I finished [work] on me birthday and I took in some
> bottles of port and sherry for the lads. About sixty or
> seventy had a glass each and I went back in the evening to
> see the night men . . . I stayed on till half past twelve and
> they all sang Happy Birthday but I really finished on the
> Friday. If you were on one shift you wouldn't see all the
> lads so I went to see all the shifts. They all wished me the
> best and I shook hands with every person there.

We had a wonderful ceremony. It was the biggest send-off
they'd had at . . . for a mere employee. We had about a
hundred people. There's a large pavilion down there and
we had a real good do . . . I was very pleased first of all to
see quite a number of people coming in from the various
factories. It was very nice and I was able to thank them all.

(Crawford, 1973, p. 453)

A more jaundiced (albeit fictional) account of a retirement
ceremony is given by Barbara Pym in her novel *Quartet in
Autumn*. In the passage reproduced below, the influences on
the conduct of the ceremony — particularly in respect of
status and organisational time — are brilliantly captured:

The organization where Letty and Marcia worked regarded
it as a duty to provide some kind of retirement party for
them, when the time came for them to give up working.
Their status as ageing unskilled women did not entitle
them to an evening party, but it was felt that a lunchtime
gathering, leading only to more than usual drowsiness in
the afternoon, would be entirely appropriate. The other
advantage of a lunchtime party was that only medium
Cyprus sherry need be provided, whereas the evening
called for more exotic and expensive drinks, wines and
even the occasional carefully concealed bottle of whisky
or gin — 'the hard stuff', as Norman called it, in his bitterness at being denied access to it. Also at lunchtime sand-
wiches could be eaten, so that there was no need to have
lunch and it was felt by some that at a time like this it was
'better' to be eating — it gave one something to do.

(Pym, 1980, p. 83)

Yet on retirement day, even if one really hated one's job,
there will almost certainly be some reasons for regret. Feelings
about 'missing the lads', missing work, all sorts of things,
will inevitably run through one's mind. Memories will be
selective as they range over forty to fifty years of work, and
the strengths rather than weaknesses of the work environment will tend to be emphasised. People will recall the support,
the encouragement and the stimulation they received from
work-mates; for one day at least the tensions and disap-

pointments will be pushed aside. Here are three car workers from the Midlands describing their final day:[3]

> When I retired I had a ruddy great lump come in me throat I couldn't help it . . . you can't help it, when you get lads like that . . . that you've been with for a long time.

> Well you're a bit jittery at leaving your work-mates . . . I went down there a week or two afterwards and had a chat with them.

> It didn't hit me until the next week on the Monday night, a lot of them come along here to go to the works and the wife and I were sat watching the television and from quarter to eight till about ten past was just one continual peep, peep, peep . . . you know the horns blowing. But on the Friday morning . . . as I came out it never hit me until I got here, the lad come round and he says to his mum: 'They gave our Dad a bloomin' good send off.' Of course, the missus broke down . . . it upset me as well then.

As these comments would suggest, the period after retirement can be a difficult one as the individual adjusts to a major change in his status. People may feel a sense of 'loss' without the routine and interest provided by work and a sense of loneliness cut off from the friendships and associations formed within the work-place. Here, for example, are comments from two car workers:

> It seemed as though you were suddenly cut off from life . . . going out of everything you've done. I was 14 when I started work and I finished when I was 65. That's 51 years of working life and you're suddenly cut off from it . . . it does have an effect on you.

> Oh! I felt terrible . . . yes. I felt lost, absolutely lost . . . didn't know what to do with meself. I was getting up at the usual time . . . I was really sometimes a bit depressed.

There will undoubtedly be many experiences like this, particularly in the early phases of retirement and among those leaving work without plans or preparation. Yet the main difficulty people will face is not a sense of boredom or frustration through being deprived of work, but bewilderment about how retirement is to be coped with, given a drastic drop in income and possibly poor health. For many workers physical decline begins in their fifties and sixties, making work more of a burden. In the United Kingdom 30—35 per cent of manual workers and 23 per cent of non-manual workers are likely to be in poor health by the age of 65 (Shephard, 1978). In a French study quoted by Carver and Rodda (1978) two groups of factory workers were studied; one with an average age of 34, the other 54. These groups were compared with groups from other social classes (e.g. teachers). The researchers found that

> deterioration characteristic of ageing was much more rapid among the factory workers: systolic blood pressure was higher, resting cardiac rhythm quicker, physical strength weaker and deterioration in intellectual ability and memory more marked. Also, the frequency of cardiovascular complaints and the use of sleeping tablets was much higher.
>
> (Carver and Rodda, 1978, p. 98)

The drop in income will also be a major factor causing anxiety in the retirement period. In a study by Age Concern (1974) 40 per cent of those with extra income above the state pension agreed a lot with the statement 'I was very happy to retire'; the figure for those without extra money was 27 per cent. For some groups of workers the reduction in income can amount to 50 per cent or more. Such a decrease will force major changes in the individual's life-style and a rapid deterioration in the quality of life. 'Retirement's all right as long as you've got money and your health', people will often say. And so it is, for without them it can become a crushing burden, a routine existence: even more routine than the working environment, from which many were glad to escape.

For the middle-class retiree, ownership of a house combined with an occupational pension can limit at least some of the constraints felt in retirement. On the other hand, the dependence of working-class people on the State pension plus either a very small occupational pension or supplementary benefit can put beyond reach the style of life achieved over the years. At an individual level the consequences of this can be highly distressing. Here are comments from two retired car workers and a retired machinist from the north-east of England:

Well . . . financially . . . that's all miserable financially . . . I have tried to think of ways round it but you're reluctant to take the chances. If it was left to me I'd do something about it . . . but I'd have to leave here to do it . . . get a mobile home for retired people or something in that line which would give me two or three thousand quid . . . a bigger margin to play with . . . a few more quid a week just to make life easier. I think any couple that's worked hard all their lives . . . they're entitled to a bottle of whisky or a bottle of brandy . . . you can't consider it these days . . . you've got to think in terms of keeping warm and having decent grub and that sort of thing . . . they are the main items. Whereas you didn't have to consider them when you were working, you had that automatically.

(retired car worker)

We used to enjoy ourselves. We thought it was great at the beginning. We went down the town, had a little drink had a bottle of Guinness . . . go in and have a meal which was cheap then about two years ago. We knew a place where we could get a nice little meal, just 15 shillings for two of us, a really good little meal. Of course I had the money to spend – the £200 [from an insurance policy] – and I had a little bit put by, but as time went on it just dwindled away. After a few months it began to get me down not having the money. But at first I thought it was great.

(retired machinist)

You've got to face it, we knew this would come up sooner or later as far as me and the wife is concerned . . . there's a lot of things as regards that we used to have . . . for instance . . . it might sound child talk to you . . . I used to think of nothing, you know, of going out and buying 2 lb of chocolates and enjoying meself, eating things like that . . . fruit and stuff . . . and then I would think nothing about going into town and bringing a crab back . . . which is all gone for a burton . . . these are some of the things. It's just like . . . it's just the ordinary day-to-day things to live on you know and . . . er . . . the luxury parts are out of it.

(retired car worker)

CLASS AND SOCIAL ACTIVITIES IN RETIREMENT

Financial constraint is not the only distinguishing mark between middle- and working-class retirees. Crawford (1972), in a study of people five months into their retirement, found important class differences in the type of roles in which people intended to be active: middle-class men intending to be more involved (than their working-class counterparts) in organisational roles. Crawford found two major patterns among men regarding anticipation of retirement: first a group composed mainly of non-manual workers who were looking forward to retirement, and who had a variety of roles outside the home; second, a group of manual workers who played few roles outside the domestic sphere and the immediate family and who were dreading their retirement.

A study by Munnichs (1969) of role patterns among retired teachers and steelworkers in the Netherlands concluded that the former had more varied and individual role activities. Research on the same occupational groups in Chicago (Bengston et al., 1969) produced similar findings to those reported by Crawford. The authors suggested that there may be some general occupational factors seen in the interplay between personality and social role which might help explain the consistent differences between the two groups of retirees (Bengston et al., 1969, p. 67).

Certainly, variations in the work environment go some way to explaining class differences in later life. Non-manual workers, for example, may learn skills and roles more easily adaptable to the retirement period. A study comparing retired architects and manual workers (Phillipson, 1978) found that the former had a range of occupational skills they were able to utilise in retirement. In some respects they straddled both sides of the mental and manual division of labour and the rounded development of skills and abilities to which this led undoubtedly made retirement both easier to adjust to and ultimately more fulfilling for the individuals concerned. The architects were not in the position of having to shed a restrictive work identity and then to assume one which was appropriate for retirement. On the contrary, they carried through both a secure self-image, and a set of skills and resources which could usefully be exploited in the post-work period. Furthermore, they saw (and felt) the advantages which retirement had for them in terms of enjoying these interests and resources within a period free of work responsibilities.

For many working-class groups, on the other hand, there is a greater degree of discontinuity between life in work and life in retirement. The factory environment itself encourages the development of a very limited range of skills, few of which have relevance beyond the factory gate. If work does have an influence on the non-work area of life, it may only be in a negative sense. People working different shifts from week to week may find it difficult to participate actively within the community; people doing assembly work may often be too tired to go out. The result of such practices may appear at their most acute in retirement, when individuals will require a far broader range of activities and relationships than their work environment may have allowed.

The impact of class differences is reflected in studies of time use among the elderly. A survey by Abrams (1978) found that in comparison with their working life professional and managerial groups actually reduce the hours spent on passive leisure activities (watching television, reading, etc.) in their retirement; unskilled workers, on the other hand, increase such activities until they consume half their waking hours. Abrams comments that:

> If we are looking to a future when there is much more time to be filled by the middle-aged and the elderly as retired people, then a strong case can be made out, on grounds of general social well-being, for introducing

working class men and women in middle age, and even earlier, to the skills, interests and values that are now enjoyed by middle class people. Very probably, these help account for the fact that the average middle class man currently outlives his working class fellow-citizen by anything up to 10 years.

(Abrams, 1978, p. 686)

LIBERATION IN RETIREMENT

Despite the pessimism expressed so far in this chapter, the positive features attached to the retirement experience should not be neglected. Increasing numbers of retirees report a sense of freedom and release from responsibility. Sadly, for the majority of pensioners, a backdrop of material hardship is ever present, but within this people are learning a sense of purpose and awareness of the advantages which retirement can bring. A survey by Age Concern (1974) found that most people find something to enjoy about their new life, freedom being the initial and strongest favourable reaction particularly amongst men. Most people in the survey reported they were just as busy in retirement as before. A study of 120 voluntary early retirees found the majority were highly satisfied with their retirement. The researchers report 85 per cent as saying they would retire early again, and many said they would have preferred to retire even earlier if the option had been available (McGoldrick and Cooper, 1980).

What, however, are the feelings and experiences behind these findings? Here are five men talking about the subjective advantages of retirement:

I reckoned I could fill my time in very nicely at home. I'm not a 'do it yourself man'. I'm not handy like that . . . there would be paintwork and all this but I thought after you have worked 50 years I think you've worked your limit . . . as long as you've got interests to keep you going . . . because my family has been away for some 18 years now, we can always have a bit of a holiday by going to see them . . . we could always put our time in that way. I reckoned after working 50 years I had worked enough.

(retired railwayman)

When I retired I was happy as anything. I knew full well I could occupy my time. There's the garden there, I could concentrate on that, and on top of that I could relax . . . I can sit here and watch the life in that garden . . . you see the finches . . . they come down when the fruit is growing . . . they have nested in the trees . . . and I've protected them from the cats. I found myself in retirement there was lots of things I wanted to do.

(retired local government worker)

Well as regards retirement . . . when a person has been underground for so many years it's a new lease of life . . . a new life . . . I've found a complete change in everything. You're not run by the clock — doing this or doing the other . . . you really feel as if you've been born again.

(retired miner)

The first year seemed to me like an extended holiday. I couldn't believe that I hadn't got to get into the rat-race and get into the office . . . that sort of thing. This was the thing I enjoyed more than anything; the first 12 months as I say was like an extended holiday . . . I could hardly believe my luck.

(retired architect)

I was very pleasantly surprised with retirement. I think partly because I . . . because I was always a little bit slow and could never catch up . . . and if that's your great anxiety — catching up — well . . . when you've no longer got to catch up it's something of a relief.

(retired architect)

The impression from these interviews — and it is confirmed in a number of studies — is the sense of release people often feel when finally leaving work. Retirement has been 'earned', a just reward for years of work from adolesence to early old age. Initial confusion there may be over how time is to be filled; beyond this, however, there is a tendency for individuals to feel it is time to let others take the strain and do the worrying.

This still leaves us, however, with a distorted image of retirement. Rarely do we have a picture of this period as a time for growth and self-development. On the contrary, ideas about retirement are still embedded in a pre-retirement consciousness: one where constraints of family, community and occupation exercise considerable force. Such social attitudes are unhelpful in assisting a process of liberation, and they are reinforced by constraints within the economy. In the early 1980s the idea of an active, purposeful retirement is being encouraged by those concerned with high rates of unemployment. But how this is to be achieved when the living standards of the elderly are so low is difficult to comprehend. On the one hand, the state appears to be saying that retirement is both healthy for the individual (by creating extra leisure time), and the state (by creating new job opportunities). On the other hand, its provision of resources is so limited that retired people can only feel their status in society is marginal. However, as we suggest below, such marginalisation may not be immediately apparent in the early stages of retirement. In this period the structure and relationships lived through prior to retirement may be sufficiently resilient to protect against the decay in living standards. Beyond these early years, however, disillusionment may set in.

THE LATE STAGES OF RETIREMENT

At the start of the retirement period, and perhaps for the next four to five years, some of the problems sketched above will be softened in their impact on daily life. Thus, for the working-class retiree, contact may be maintained with former work-mates and friendships developed outside the work-place. Small amounts of savings may also be used to cushion the drop in weekly or monthly income. In the period beyond this, however, critical changes will occur in the individual's social network and in his or her financial position. The inevitable death of close friends and spouse can generate feelings of loneliness and depression (and fears of one's own future death). Financial constraints may also cause great bitterness: income shows a very real statistical decline with age — particularly after age 75. The individual may feel bewildered and estranged from a world where living standards are moving far beyond their own. Gladys Elder, in her moving study of old age, writes:

> I find there is an underlying feeling of loneliness in the aged, of being left behind, of having been cheated. There is a feeling of bitterness, of helplessness, and in many cases an incredible stoicism displayed in face of economic difficulties and physical disabilities; a valiant attempt to retain some dignity, in many cases by an appearance of not caring. Then, too, the old are resigned in the face of a defeat they cannot possibly hope to reverse. For their very circumstances make them helpless, as do frustration, the discomforts and disabilities of the aging process, the economic shackles and the indignities to which they are subjected.
>
> (Elder, 1977, p. 34)

Physical and health problems became increasingly important for the later age groups. Hunt's (1978) survey reported that of the more mobile elderly men (those who are neither bedfast or housebound), only 37 per cent of those aged 75 to 89 had no disability. In this age group 16 per cent suffered from arthritis or rheumatism, 15 per cent from a cardiac condition, 8.4 per cent from blindness or failing sight.

As far as the very elderly are concerned, we are just beginning to learn about their daily round of activities. Social isolation is one inevitable accompaniment to late old age. Abrams (1978), in his study of the elderly in four urban areas, found men becoming progressively less gregarious beyond age 75, the loss of close friends and the effect of moving into a predominantly female world both having important influences. A later report from this survey explored the use of time by the very elderly. Television-watching consumes a large portion of the day in later life (particularly among men living alone). People reported increases in the time spent 'just resting' — two hours daily being spent in this way. Social-class differences in time use maintained their importance. Compared with the working-class elderly, the middle-class elderly spent less time watching television, were less prone to join clubs for old people and filled their leisure time with a wider range of activities (Abrams, 1980).

In terms of family ties changes towards greater isolation seem to occur beyond age 75. In the survey by Abrams, of men living alone in this age band, 34 per cent report seeing their family either a little or a lot less compared with five years ago. Hunt found that men were rather less likely than women to have visits from adult grandchildren and nephews and nieces. For both men and women aged 75 or over daughters in law and sons in law are the most frequent visitors (Abrams, 1980, p. 39, Hunt, 1978, p. 96).

However, the minority experiences should also be noted. In Hunt's study 6 per cent of men aged 75—84 never received a visit from a relative; 7 per cent had no living close relatives (Hunt, 1978).

With the expansion in the very elderly population now taking place, we urgently need more knowledge about the range of experiences behind these statistics. The work of Blythe (1979) has provided us with some powerful descriptions of old age. Here are fragments from two interviews, the first with a retired civil engineer (aged 75), the second a retired farrier (aged 82):

I am rather amazed that I have survived. My eldest brother was such a terribly fit person that it was he who should have survived, yet he got cancer a few months ago and went. He was famously fit, the active, charming, kindly one, the handsome one, the popular one. And now he has died and it has shaken me. It has been a most shattering experience for me. I saw him as always well but during his last illness the doctor and all sorts of people talked of his being 'a good age', and things like that. If he was a good age, and popular and strong, as I thought, then what am I? I am not a good age, I am old. That's the truth of the matter. And this thought has changed me. All at once I have an awful lot to do and must do it quickly. It is as though my brother was saying, 'If I can go, who was so perfect and popular, then how much longer can it be for you? So I am systematically working my way through everything because I am now the head of the family and I must.

(Blythe, 1979, p. 260)

I don't know where I would have found more happiness than at the forge. It's all shut up now and I sit an' listen to the kittle b'ilin' or watch the telly. I find the time passes well enough but occasionally, well, I feel on my own. All on my own. There are some days when I don't see a soul to speak to — although there is plenty goo by. My wife, she died four years agoo. That's her picture up there. It's an oil paintin' by our kind neighbour. At the bottom right-hand corner there is a little glimpse of my forge. At the time I did properly miss my wife, and no mistake, but I had my daughters and that took it off. When you've spent your whol' life a-usin' of your hands, like I have, you don't know what to do when you can't. You really don't. I have two nice daughters and grandsons that are gittin' on well . . . I balance things up when I can. I've got no work and no wife, but I've got what I've done, haven't I? We've all got that, haven't we?

(Blythe, 1979, p. 76)

CAPITALISM AND RETIREMENT

We have concentrated so far on how individuals (albeit from different social classes) have adapted to retirement. In doing this we are following a tradition in sociological studies of retirement, one which has tended to isolate reactions to retirement from broader aspects of the economy and society. Friedmann and Orbach, in a major review of the literature on retirement argue, that:

Without ignoring the real problems retirement poses, it is of little benefit to treat these uncritically as inherent in the presumed nature of retirement, apart from the actual nature of the circumstances that surround the event of retirement, the process of retiring, and the character of

retirement living. Reviewing the results of research on
retirement demonstrates the consistent manner in which
the blinding effect of biases have served to attribute to
'retirement' consequences that are the result of poor
health, inadequate income provisions, aspects of the individual's total life experiences, and general problems that
face our society as a whole.

(Friedmann and Orbach, 1974, p. 625)

In the concluding section I shall approach the problem
posed by Friedmann and Orbach through an examination of
the relationship between the capitalist mode of production
and experiences in retirement. A major theme in the argument
will be that we are witnessing a conflict between two
dominant trends in capitalism: first, the rationalisation and
fragmentation of work processes; second, the increased availability of free time beyond the work situation. The contradiction between these trends is that while work within capitalism is becoming ever more limited in its capacity to expand
and develop human potential, the expansion in educational,
leisure and cultural activities is providing a framework for
this potential to be realised. However, until work is more
closely related to individual needs and capacities, the benefits
arising from such activities are likely to be wasted.[4]
The influence of capitalist production on the individual
has been an important strand in Marxist writing. Sève, for
example, suggests that it is in the essence of capitalist society
to

stand in the way of the indefinitely expanded reproduction
of capacities in the majority of individuals, because one
of its most basic traits is to transform labour-power into
a commodity and to pay it *at its value*, in other words
according to the *minimal* conditions of its production and
reproduction: in this respect, well before biological sen-
escence indirectly comes into play, capitalist relations
exercise an unceasing retarding influence . . .

It is because it separates the individual from the productive forces, converts man himself into a commodity,
founds social enrichment on the stealing of the labour-

time and of the free-time of the vast majority, that capitalism ossifies and dichotomises personalities to their inner-
most.

(Sève, 1978, pp. 362, 365)

This theme has been explored at a more empirical level by
researchers in the sociology of work. Numerous writers have
pointed to the deteriorating quality of the work environment,
with the thrust towards de-skilling and the reduction in scope
for decision-making by office and factory workers (for a
summary of the literature see Salaman, 1981). Other writers
(most notably Sennett and Cobb, 1973) have pointed to the
psychological damage which work inflicts. People, they
suggest, come to feel that the repetitive jobs which they perform are a true reflection of their worth, and that their
position in the social hierarchy is a reasonable indicator of
their skills and abilities.

Because of the divorce between the sociology and the political economy of retirement, the implications of these trends
have rarely been considered by students of retirement behaviour. The argument to be put forward in this study is that, by
limiting the access of workers to education throughout their
lives and by institutionalising the division between mental
and manual labour, the capitalist mode of production creates
tensions and contradictions in the way workers experience
retirement. Marx observes that 'The worker feels himself at
home only during his leisure, whereas at work he feels home-
less' (Bottomore and Rubel, 1974, p. 177). Retirement, however, is still affected by this alienation within the work-place.
The capitalist mode of production allows workers to develop
only a limited range of skills (for some, none at all); it encourages methods of work (extensive overtime, continental
shift systems) which make it difficult for workers to develop
as individuals. When they retire — quite suddenly — they
have the chance to do (they are told) all those things which
work allowed no time for. But the contradictions are these:
an active retirement depends on financial security, yet over
60 per cent of retired people in Britain live in households
which are below, or very close to, the official poverty line; it
requires a certain degree of health, yet one-third of manual

workers retire in a poor state of health; it requires a range of educational and cultural facilities, yet present cuts in public expenditure are severely reducing opportunities in adult education and the university system.

These tendencies are a good illustration of the central contradiction in capitalism between the *forces of production* and the *relations of production*. Gough describes this contradiction in the following way:

> Writing on the impact of modern machinery, Marx describes how, on the one hand, it shatters the traditional division of labour, extends people's control over nature, creates a need for the more rounded development of the worker; yet under capitalism it actually increases insecurity, reduces the individual's control over the labour process, fragments this process and increases the division of labour.
>
> (Gough, 1979, pp. 11–12)

A similar point could be made about retirement. Thus, while capitalism has created the preconditions for retirement in advance of physiological decline, it turns this period into one of insecurity or even crisis. This feeling of insecurity reflects the division between work and life, a division that has become the hallmark of industrial and monopoly capitalism. This area has been explored by E. P. Thompson in his essay 'Time, Work Discipline and Industrial Capitalism' (1967). Thompson shows how the work pattern evolved from alternating bouts of intense labour and bouts of idleness to one where wage-labour forced the regularisation of hours and the internalisation of a work discipline. This internalisation was such that

> by the 1830s and 1840s it was commonly observed that the English industrial worker was marked off from his fellow Irish worker not by a greater capacity for hard work, but by his regularity, his methodical paying out of energy, and perhaps also by a repression, not of enjoyment but of the capacity to relax in the old, uninhibited ways.
>
> (Thompson, 1967, p. 91)

This new rhythm of labour involved new time valuations, time itself became a commodity, a value and a source of wealth. Time which was lost became lost wealth, and lost opportunity. 'Putting one's time in' henceforth became part of the process concerned with the expansion of value. (It is significant that in talking to people after retirement, this phrase, 'putting in one's time', recurs constantly, activities being viewed not as ends in themselves but as a means of filling time). Thompson goes on to suggest that

> If we are to have enlarged leisure in an automated future, the problem is not 'how are we going to *consume* all these additional time units of leisure?' but 'what will be the capacity for experience of the men who have this undirected time to live'. If we maintain a puritan time valuation, a commodity valuation, then it is a question of how this time is put to *use*, or how it is exploited by the leisure industries. But if the purposive notation of time-use becomes less compulsive, then men might have to re-learn some of the arts of living lost in the Industrial Revolution: how to fill the interstices of their days with enriched, more leisurely personal and social relations; how to break down and move the barriers between work and life.
>
> (Thompson, 1967, p. 95)

Institutionalised retirement, following the above, involves the search for 'new' approaches to the use of time, one aspect of the discontinuous nature of retirement being the limitations inherent in existing commodity valuations of time. The latter was developed in the struggle between capital and labour for control over the work process. With monopoly capitalism we have reached the furthest point in the process whereby

> every step in the labor process is divorced so far as possible, from special knowledge and training and reduced to simple labor. Meanwhile, the relatively few persons for whom special knowledge and training are reserved are freed so far as possible from the obligations of simple labor. In this way, a structure is given to all labor processes that at its

extremes polarizes those whose time is infinitely valuable and those whose time is worth almost nothing.
(Braverman, 1974, pp. 82–3)

Such a polarisation raises some difficult questions about the possibilities for incorporating retirement into work and life. For example, we might consider a major reorganisation of work itself. Instead of the present demarcations which run through the labour market (particularly those formed around age and gender), a situation might be envisaged where a worker could enter and re-enter the work-force at a number of points in his or her work career (with facilities for sabbaticals, paid educational leave, etc.). In this situation work and education would be seen to have complementary functions throughout the individual's life span. Where, in addition, workers had control over conditions of employment, the pace of work, etc., the retention of the older employee would be much easier. Conversely, the acceptance of a positive interaction between work, education and leisure would also make retirement much easier.

The kind of changes discussed above will, however, be difficult to implement without radical changes in the distribution of power and control at work and the subversion of the existing division between mental and manual labour. Radical changes in the way people experience retirement can only come, therefore, when there have been major changes in the experience of work. Gorz has made a similar point in relation to leisure:

Leisure activity can be no more than a compensation and a way of passing the time, with no cultural (and therefore social) relevance, until it has found an extension, an outlet, and a practical application, in the most important of all social activities — namely, work. So long as this while continuing to govern social relations, excludes, represses, or discourages the free extension of individual faculties, culture will tend to remain a private luxury, an abstract adornment, and the negation of the real social individual not his fulfilment.
(Gorz, 1974, p. 202)

In conclusion, I have tried to situate retirement within the context of the capitalist mode of production. I have suggested that the institutionalisation of retirement creates demands for a restructuring of the work career. I would also argue that the increase in the number of elderly people raises questions about how production is organized: How, for example, can work be arranged to assist people in preparing for a period such as retirement? How can the rights of older workers be safeguarded?

Finally, institutionalised retirement raises questions about the relationship between work and leisure. It might be argued that the alienating character of work had less consequences when the 'non-work' area was so limited (because of lower life expectancy, massive amounts of overtime, etc.). However, given that retirement has become more significant for the working class, the influence of work on other spheres of the individual's life is of increased significance. When work is experienced as oppressive and stultifying then the impact of this on a period such as retirement (a man of 60 can expect to live for another fifteen years) can no longer be ignored.

5

Women in Retirement and Old Age

In the previous chapter I attempted to develop an alternative to the conventional view of the male's experience of retirement. I tried to relate the analysis both to the class and occupational structure and to aspects of work organisation within capitalism. In doing this I tried to move away from viewing retirement solely in terms of individual adjustment. The concern of this next chapter is to attempt a similar analysis for women, exploring the conventional view that, in comparison with men, they experience greater security and continuity in the period of old age. Simone de Beauvoir has presented this image in the following way:

In the immense majority of cases, being suddenly flung from the active into the inactive category, being classed as old, and undergoing a frightening drop in income and standard of living is a tragedy that has serious psychological and spiritual consequences. It is men who feel the effect most. Women live longer, and it is the very aged solitary women who make up the most underprivileged stratum of the population; yet generally speaking the elderly woman adapts herself to her stage better than her husband. She is the person who runs the home, and in this her position is the same as that of the peasants and craftsmen of former times — for her, too, work and life merge into one another. No decree from without suddenly cuts her activity short. It does grow less from the time her grown-up children leave the home and this crisis, which often happens quite early in life, often disturbs her very badly; but still she

does not see herself thrown into total idleness and her role
of grandmother brings her fresh possibilities.
                    (Simone de Beauvoir, 1972, pp. 261–2)

This theme has found support in historical and sociological
studies and in general works on old age.[1] Too often, however,
these studies have relied upon assertion rather than detailed
analysis of the experiences of older women. I would argue
that if such an analysis were undertaken a bleaker and more
troubled view of women in later life would emerge. In this
chapter I shall examine distinctive pressures affecting the
daily lives of older women, relating their existence to conditions both within the home and in paid employment. The
form in which I shall present the analysis will differ from that
of the previous chapter because of:

(a) the limited material available on older women (an aspect
     to be discussed in the following section); and
(b) the different economic and sociological constraints
     operating on the lives of older women, as compared
     with men.

THE POSITION OF OLDER WOMEN IN WOMEN'S STUDIES

The limited interest in the fate of older women is the first
major issue which must be tackled. In the 60-plus age group
women outnumber men by 50 per cent. Among those over
75 they comprise nearly 70 per cent of the total. Despite
this, it has been the problems which *men* experience in retirement and in old age which have concentrated the minds of
policy-makers and researchers. In the relevant research literature few studies have bothered to explore the reactions of
wives to their husbands' retirement.[2] Crawford has commented upon the 'almost total lack of studies in this area' (1971,
p. 256), and a similar point could be made concerning, for
example, single women, older women workers, widowhood,
the menopause, and so on.[3] So total has the neglect of women
in later life been that a recent survey (Delamont, 1981) of
research on women secures only nine pages for older women
in a text of nearly 250 pages. Typically, these pages are the

least illuminating in the whole book, and appear virtually as an afterthought to the discussion of the 'real' issues facing women.

Two major factors seem to account for this lack of interest. First, in the growth of feminist groups and literature, primary emphasis was given to problems of oppression facing younger women in the home and the work-place. The issues touched upon included: (a) the problems of combining housework with paid work outside the home; (b) the isolation involved in caring for children; (c) the violence against women within and outside the home; (d) problems of low pay and limited opportunities at work; and (e) the politics of reproduction. Although older women were deeply affected by many of these issues, connections across the life-cycle were rarely explored in political campaigns or in research. The assumption drawn was that the key problems facing women were principally those affecting women in their twenties and thirties. This viewpoint was reinforced by a second factor which occasionally surfaced in the writing and propaganda of the women's movement: namely, the hostility and resentment expressed towards older women. Rowbotham (1973) reported seeing her female elders 'as creatures sunk into the very deadening circumstances from which I was determined to escape'. She spoke of feeling that 'they seemed always to want to damp you down and hold you in' (1973, p. 12). From another perspective, an older activist in the women's movement found that

women often resent me and criticise me, or worse, avoid me, because I am their mother's generation. A writers' evening held publicly late in 1978 devoted a sizeable portion of its content to relationships between mothers and daughters. In every case, the mother was at fault.

(Long, 1979, p. 16)

The continued growth and development of the women's movement, combined with the ageing of its own members, is likely to lead to a softening in these attitudes (a phenomenon which can already be observed in the case of the American women's movement). However, significant changes are unlikely to occur until the links between the experiences of older and younger women are better understood. In the following sections of this chapter a start will be made on unravelling connections between these different age groups.

WOMEN AS WORKERS

1. *Domestic labour*

The lack of research on women in later life is usually justified in terms of retirement from work being a less significant event for women, and in terms of their having a number of other duties which can be maintained after leaving paid work. Very rarely have researchers seen these duties – in particular those connected with the care and support of other family members – as capable of producing their own conflicts and tensions. By contrast, I shall argue that women's domestic and work responsibilities may cause considerable stress in middle age and beyond.

As regards their domestic role, women have been defined as principal agents in the maintenance and reproduction of labour power. By this is meant all those duties concerned with supporting the existing work-force and preparing the next generation of workers. In fulfilling this role, women's identity has, as Oakley (1974) has observed, become closely tied to the care of children. However, it is important to remember that a combination of increased life expectancy and lower family size means that women today only spend a small proportion of their lives actively caring for their own children. The role of the woman (mother) as the central caring figure has, none the less, been retained. Indeed, we see it being extended to embrace a variety of social contexts. Thus, on a formal level, women comprise the majority of home helps, nurses and volunteers (WRVS, etc.). Informally they are the main agents within the family concerned with the care of the sick and elderly; historically this is hardly new, but demographic pressures have increased the range of demands made upon women (Phillipson, 1981).

The key point, therefore, is that the caring role allocated

to women may be moved to various points in the life-cycle. As a consequence, even if a woman wishes to break away from the caring role, institutional support (in the form of work opportunities, day-care facilities for elderly parents, etc.) may be very limited. Indeed, social policies towards women are currently intensifying the pressure upon them to assume formal or informal caring roles wherever possible (Finch and Groves, 1980).

Thus, as women reach middle and early old age they may experience a range of new restrictions affecting their lives. Many will, in fact, find themselves involved in supportive and caring roles at least as intense as those experienced at earlier stages of the life cycle. One of the most recent surveys on the experience of caring for elderly and handicapped people (Equal Opportunities Commission, 1980) found that women were key figures in providing support. The survey discovered that responsibility for caring for an elderly or handicapped relative increased with age, reaching a peak around 50, i.e. precisely when, after bringing up a family, many women are looking for activities outside the home. Kirk (1980), in her work as a tutor and counsellor with the Open University, has found that many mature female students have their studies disrupted by the infirmity or sickness of elderly relatives. She writes:

When a family crisis is prolonged, it is usually a daughter, not a son, who is called upon to take care of, and even nurse, the aged relative. Even if a women is working full-time, her career is still regarded as dispensable (unlike that of her husband or brother), and she is likely to be the only one with the time and skill to nurse a sick relative.

(Kirk, 1980, p. 120)

Supporting an elderly person may make considerable demands on the physical strength of the carer. Added to this, however, is the psychological impact of support for a mother or close relative who may soon die. Simone de Beauvoir (1966) discusses this theme at some length in her book *A Very Easy Death*. Describing her mother's terminal illness, she writes:

> The knowledge that because of her age my mother's life
> must soon come to an end did not lessen the horrible
> surprise: she had sarcoma. Cancer, thrombosis, pneumonia:
> it is as violent and unforeseen as an engine stopping in the
> middle of the sky. My mother encouraged one to be
> optimistic when, crippled with arthritis and dying, she
> asserted the infinite value of each instant; but her vain
> tenaciousness also ripped and tore the reassuring curtain
> of everyday triviality. There is no such thing as a natural
> death: nothing that happens to man is ever natural, since
> his presence calls the world into question. All men must
> die: but for every man his death is an accident and, even if
> he knows it and consents to it, an unjustifiable violation.
>   (Simone de Beauvoir, 1966, pp. 105–6)

As well as watching the decline of her own parents, the older
women may also spend a significant part of her life caring for
a sick husband. We noted in the previous chapter the large
numbers of men who retire in a poor state of health, and it is
often forgotten that the burden for their care will almost
inevitably fall upon the wife. Puner (1978) has argued that
the stresses provoked by this care may haunt the survivor
because of compassion for the sufferer, or because of guilt
feelings over not having done enough to help. Moreover, the
burden of this care will inevitably increase where (a) family
ties are weakened through social and geographical mobility,
and (b) medical and welfare facilities are withdrawn or
reduced as a result of cuts in public expenditure.

2. *Wage labour*

We have already seen that in their domestic role women are
central figures both as regards the maintenance and reproduction of current and future labour, and also in support for
those no longer involved in the productive system. Along-
side this, however, we must consider the role played by
women in paid work. The postwar period has seen a dramatic
increase in women workers in the age group 45-plus (two-

thirds of married women and nearly three-quarters of non-married women aged 45 to 59 are economically active). This development reflects important changes in fertility and family life. Writing of the 1950s, Elizabeth Wilson has noted:

> Whereas once women had produced a large number of children and had started having their children later in life, now they started young and completed their families very early. Once, women had had only a few years of life left to them after the last child had left the nest; now many women had completed childbearing by about the age of forty and could look forward to twenty or thirty more years of life. They were therefore more and more looking for work to fill those years. Subsequently 'women's dual role' was virtually elevated into a principle. Henceforward there was to be a generational drive, with the younger women in the wife-and-mother category, and the older in the returning-to-work role. These older women workers would often be both part-time and unskilled, to fit in with their diminished but not extinguished domestic responsibilities; to fit in, too, with a shortage of unskilled labour.
>
> (Wilson, 1980, p. 48)

Much of the work carried out by women is in the poorer-paid, less skilled, auxiliary occupations. Even within similar occupations women are usually paid much less than men. In addition, social attitudes to working women have continued to emphasise the secondary nature of their work role. Commenting on the 74 per cent increase in female unemployment between May 1979 and November 1980, Peters and Weston argue:[4]

> It is no coincidence that the loss of women's role has been accompanied by advice from the Social Services Secretary Patrick Jenkin that women should stay at home . . . and not take jobs away from men in the paid sector of the economy. . . Meanwhile the burden to care for the sick and old and provide free domestic labour is back on women as public services are cut.
>
> (Peters and Weston, 1981, p. 41)

FEMALE LABOUR UNDER CAPITALISM: SOME IMPLICATIONS
FOR LATER LIFE

Women may experience various forms of discrimination
around the time of retirement, many of which stem directly
from conditions attached to their work at home and in
employment. In the area of paid work, a woman may find
her own career being sacrificed through problems in the
family or because of her husband's retirement. Parker (1980)
found that the health of other family members was an important factor influencing a woman's retirement. Crawford (1972),
in her Bristol study, found that manual workers' wives were
more likely than the wives of non-manual workers to give
up their jobs on their husband's retirement. She argues that
this may reflect 'differences in class-related norms concerning
appropriate sex roles within the family': 'In working class
marriages a stricter division of labour is reported and to reverse
the roles completely with the husband at home and the wife
out at work may be flouting the norms beyond toleration'
(1972, p. 224).

Because women are viewed as marginal to the labour force,
very few attempts have been made to look at the problems
they may experience in leaving paid work. This is particularly
noticeable in the area of retirement preparation courses,
where, in terms of membership and course content, the needs
of women part-time workers (and housewives) have been
virtually ignored. However, precisely because they are clus-
tered in unskilled, low-paid work, women may experience
serious difficulties in the transition to retirement. Parker
(1980) found single, early retired women under considerable
financial pressure, with very few receiving occupational pensions and as many as three-quarters receiving means-tested
assistance. Hunt's (1978) survey of the non-institutionalised
elderly found that 45.5 per cent of men, compared with
20.3 per cent of women, received a pension from a former
employer or spouse's employer; 34.3 per cent of women, compared with 20.5 per cent of men, had had recourse to a
supplementary pension.

The problems faced by women in retirement are further
complicated if we consider the full-time housewife. The social

isolation accompanying housework has been a persistent theme in women's studies.[5] Hobson has summarised it in the following way:

> The location of women's domestic labour and reproduction of the agents of labour power, within the privatized sphere of the home, has meant that for women there is neither a physical nor an emotional separation of the sphere of work and leisure. The privatized nature of housework which necessitates the isolation of the individual woman in the home is one of the most recognizable sites of her oppression. The male wage labourer returns to the private sphere of his home to be 'reproduced' in a fit state for work the next day. This period away from work can be seen as the time when the wage labourer has leisure time. However, there is no space for leisure for women at the same time. The woman works in the home during the day when the man is at work but when he returns from work, she still has to work.
>
> (Hobson, 1978, p. 88)

Retirement studies have rarely been sensitive to these characteristics of housework. As a result, researchers viewed with genuine surprise the findings of a number of studies conducted in the 1960s and 1970s indicating that in comparison with men women in paid work were more resistant to retirement.[6] The reasons for these results are still not entirely clear, but there is evidence to suggest that when recalling the boredom and lack of companionship experienced at home, women may give extra priority to the social ties formed within the work-place. This may be reinforced by what Jacobsohn (1974), in a study of semi-skilled male and female workers, has described as a process of 'anticipatory widowhood'. The women in his sample looked ahead to a period of loneliness and isolation with the death of their husbands. Given this perspective, they expressed greater attachment than men to relationships formed within the work-place. Jacobsohn linked his findings to changes within urban society:

> one may ... speculate that the tendency among older

women in this study to prefer to remain employed is consonant with a more general trend . . . It could be tentatively suggested, for example, that this tendency is embedded in certain broad social changes. These it seems, are not entirely incompatible with a life style among females of the same strata as our respondents — one that is less decisively centred on the home and its diminishing range of social options. Among the changes of which it is possible to think in this context are redevelopment of urban areas; greater social heterogeneity of neighbourhoods; gradual dissolution of 'traditional' tightly knit social networks based on kinship and locality; increased residential mobility; elderly people's frequent physical separation from the main body of their kin; and a re-assessment of middle-aged and elderly women's roles, both in their own eyes and on the normative and institutional level.

(Jacobsohn, 1974, p. 491)

These findings were supported in Crawford's research. She found a group of women, mostly the wives of manual workers, who were involved in activities outside the home and who were dreading retirement:

Their activities were split between home and family and the outside world or were centred on the community and their friendships. They had re-engaged or re-aligned after their children left home and had forged a new life for themselves which did not depend for satisfaction on the presence of children, sibs, or husbands. It is clear from other data that they felt this kind of life threatened by retirement.

(Crawford, 1972, p. 234)

The advent of retirement may bring, as the above quotation suggests, important changes to the running of the home. For the full-time housewife there will be significant changes to her often solitary life-style. For those women with few social contacts their partner's retirement may bring some relief from loneliness (particularly where the pattern of life has been disturbed by shiftwork).[7] In other cases, where work has been stressful and hazardous (the experience of miners' wives is a good example), retirement may relieve considerable pressure on the couple's relationship. On the other hand, for women who have relationships beyond the home, the male's retirement may be perceived as threatening this wider involvement, and this may give rise to considerable tension. Finally, conflict may arise where the division of labour between partners has been particularly strict. Townsend's (1957) Bethnal Green study in the 1950s gave some vivid examples of this, as did Crawford's work some twenty years later. She found many wives worrying about the consequences of the husband's continual presence in the home:

> Some were just vaguely worried by the prospect of sharing the house with their husbands, as if the house had become their exclusive territory during the day: 'Well I just don't like the idea of having him home all day long, that's all. I'll be honest, no I wouldn't and that's the honest truth.' Others were dreading the possibility of their husbands taking over some part of their own housewife role.
>
> (Crawford, 1971, p. 270)

To set against this, where the relationship has been more open, retirement may be welcomed as a period where the couple's range of activities can be significantly increased. For such couples, retirement may lead to a considerable strengthening in their relationship in the absence of the daily pressures and tensions which often accompany work. By contrast, where — as for most working-class couples — retirement leads to a severe drop in income, it may be extremely difficult for the relationship to develop in any meaningful way.

WOMEN IN OLD AGE

In moving the discussion to the age group of 70 and beyond, the lives of women reveal areas of both dramatic change and continuity. Much of what happens to women as they reach old age appears to mark a radical break from their previous way of life. The death of partners, the movement and mobility of families and the impact of chronic illness appear to confirm old age as a period of loss and abandonment. The contribution made by social institutions (the family apart) to this experience has rarely been considered in studies examining the problems of elderly people. On the contrary, social institutions are often depicted as powerless in the face of demographic pressure. I would argue, however, that the role they play and the ideologies they hold about older women have a major influence. Many of the problems women face are not, in fact, due to the effects of physical ageing or to the shock of losing a partner, but to the restricted opportunities available to them after they have performed productive/reproductive roles. These restrictions are compounded via the low income and sex role conditioning which women bring into old age. These important examples of *continuity* in the lives of older women will be examined in the final section of this chapter.

A PROFILE OF THE OLDER WOMAN

Moving into the upper-age groups the social world becomes almost exclusively female. Among the 'old' elderly, for example (those aged 75 and over), women outnumber men by more than two to one. Not surprisingly, the experience of living alone (usually as a consequence of widowhood) is increasingly common for older women. The length of time spent alone can be quite dramatic. Hunt's (1978) survey found that 29 per cent of women aged 75–84 lived alone, 44 per cent of these having done so for more than twenty years. Abrams's (1980) survey of the elderly in four urban areas found that feelings of loneliness, depression and alienation were much more widespread among elderly women living on their own.

The problems which arise through living without a partner will be reinforced by both economic factors and physical disability. The poverty experienced by older women makes them less able to afford commodities (cars, telephones, etc.) which can assist communication. As regards physical disability, Hunt's (1978) survey details the range of health

problems affecting older women. Among more mobile
elderly women (those who are neither bedfast nor housebound), only 32.9 per cent of the 75–84-year-olds had no
disability; 27.4 per cent had arthritis or rheumatism; 16.1 per
cent a cardiac condition; and 11.3 per cent blindness or
failing sight (1978, p. 71).

We have, as yet, only a limited idea of what this information means for the daily lives of older women. We do possess
fascinating accounts of community-building among women
in later life, accounts which are illustrative of the range of
relationships older women can form (Hochschild, 1978). We
also have some distressing accounts of life inside old people's
homes (Newton, 1980). We know less, however, about what
the isolated, non-institutionalised elderly do with their time.
Evidence from the 1977 *General Household Survey* suggests
joining clubs and societies is a popular outlet for older widows
(though this may be more characteristic of working-class than
middle-class widows). Abrams's (1980) survey has provided
valuable details about the use of time by elderly men and
women. However, much more work must be done, particularly
in understanding the experiences of women in their seventies,
eighties and beyond. Moreover, the expanding empirical data
need to be more firmly related to theories about the position
of women in a capitalist society, and the interrelationship
with experiences in later life.

Finally, women, through sheer longevity, are much more
likely than men to spend their last years in some form of
institution. Among women over 85, some 12 per cent are in
old people's homes, with a further 6 per cent confined to a
hospital. The quality of life experienced by long-term residents is still a question of urgent concern. Evers (1981), for
example, has documented the 'depersonalisation' affecting
female patients in geriatric wards. Norman (1980) has noted
the authoritarian regimes within institutions and the lack of
choice or control over key areas of life such as diet, times of
sleeping, personal clothing, etc. The fact that women far
outnumber men in old people's homes may in itself to some
extent explain the low standards of care and privacy: degrada-
tion on the 'inside' reflecting external beliefs about the rights
of women in general, and elderly women in particular.

CONTINUITIES IN LATER LIFE

In presenting the above profile, we have deliberately emphasised changes which occur in the lives of older women. Yet,
as has already been argued, many of the experiences reported
by older women reveal patterns of conditioning and discrimination which have their roots in earlier phases of the
life-cycle. This is illustrated particularly well if we consider
an experience affecting the lives of virtually all married
women: that of widowhood. The response a woman makes
to losing a partner will reflect a variety of factors. A powerful role will be played by income, health and family support;
less obviously, however, an important role will be played by
attitudes and skills developed by the woman through the
period of socialisation. If this period has effected an impression of her inferiority to men, of her relative inability to
handle public affairs or administer the family budget, then it
is hardly surprising that widowhood may trigger a downward
spiral of withdrawal and social isolation. Lopata, in a major
American study of widowhood, states:

> [A] reason for the lack of involvement in service supports
> is the traditional sex-segregated nature of everyday Ameri-
> can life. Almost no women help anyone with care of an
> automobile nor do they assist on legal problems or with
> household repairs. These are tasks that fall into the man's
> domain in the usual familial division of responsibility. If
> widows do perform such services, the recipients are most
> likely their parents or friends, people with even less ex-
> perience in these areas. The widows also are not providers
> of transportation, since being unfamiliar with cars, they
> usually get rid of theirs after the death of the husband.
> Hence, they also do not need help in the case of a car —
> another consequence of a sex-segregated society.
>
> (Lopata, 1979, pp. 78–9)

The full impact of this segregation and conditioning may
only appear in the final part of the woman's life. The likelihood of her spending a major part of those years living on
her own is very high. On the positive side, being alone may

generate, as Stott (1973) has described, a new experience of freedom, and Butler and Lewis (1973) have noted that many women who were forced into marriage by cultural and family pressures might have been happier single, as career or professional women. Other older women, they suggest, may be lesbians who have been hiding as heterosexual for a life-time and who might be willing to 'come out' if the climate were favourable. Where, on the other hand, the woman lacks economic resources and/or where her confidence is low, the possibility of exercising her new found freedom may be very limited. Here, for example, is one widow describing her everyday life:

When Mrs Seymour gave up her job, there were three phases through which time filtered. When her husband was working there was the cooking and the entertaining and being with her only daughter.

Then he retired from British Rail. 'We didn't plan anything; we just lived. We did the most trivial things in the most satisfactory way.' They read, or listened to music or travelled, or walked in Regents Park . . . His last fatal illness abruptly brought in a wilderness of days where before there had been a profusion.

'Now there is the feeling that you're on the slippery slope to nothingness. I get up at six, I make a tray with tea, brush my teeth. Put on the radio for the seven o'clock news and stay in bed for three quarters of an hour. Then I get up and have breakfast. [Usually] I try to telephone someone, just to hear a voice. Nathalie usually rings me and says "What are you doing today Mum?" And I try to tell her that I've got a busy day.'

(*The Guardian*, 18 June 1980)

CONCLUDING COMMENTS

The restrictions on women in old age have increased in the early 1980s' crisis of cuts in public expenditure. Among women over 80, nine out of ten are widowed, and many live on or around the poverty line. For such women, reductions in social security and changes in the rules governing benefits can cause immense hardship. For older women with elderly mothers or fathers, the cutting of services such as home helps and meals on wheels (see Chapter 6) can mean a considerable increase in their daily work-load (this at a time when there may be increased tension and pressure in the household because of unemployment). A recent research paper on the elderly by the health service union COHSE observed that

> Those who say that children no longer care forget that longevity itself has put a new strain on families. 12 per cent of admissions to geriatric hospitals are for those whose families cannot cope any longer. They may have been worn out by the strain of eternal vigilance over a mentally confused person, by sleepless nights and perpetually clearing up after the doubly incontinent.
>
> (COHSE, 1981, p. 6)

Unfortunately, as we shall see in the following chapters, it may be some time before this pressure on women is likely to be lifted.

6

State Legislation and the Elderly

INTRODUCTION

In Chapter 3 it was argued that the growth in the elderly population had posed important dilemmas concerning the national distribution of economic resources. It was suggested that despite the emergence of retirement, there remained a flexible policy concerning the socially acceptable time to retire, the acceptability of retirement shifting with changes in the economy, assumptions about the 'burden' of elderly people, and changes in the supply of young 'productive' workers. In this chapter I wish to examine how these changes have affected social policies towards older people. Can similar movements be traced in the emergence of a concept of care and support for older people as has been identified in the case of retirement? Have policies of care developed by consensus and evolutionary growth, or has their emergence been marked by contradiction and dissension?[1]

The period to be studied will be that from the late 1940s up to the present time. The main reason for concentrating on this period is that during these years the state has come to play a significant role in the lives of older people. The National Health Act of 1946 and the National Assistance Act of 1948 were both regarded as heralding major changes in the quality of life enjoyed by the elderly. The workhouse was to be swept away and all trace of the Poor Law removed. The Ministry of Health, in its annual report of 1948–9, proclaimed the new spirit in ringing tones:

> The workhouse is doomed. Instead, Local Authorities are busy planning and opening small, comfortable homes,

where old people, many of them lonely, can live pleasantly and with dignity. The old 'master and inmate' relationship is being replaced by one more nearly approaching that of a hotel manager and his guest.

(Cited in Townsend, 1962, p. 32)

Unfortunately, the state, in the role of 'hotel manager', was to change its policies on numerous occasions in the following years. The guests could be forgiven for feeling unwelcome visitors, as the management made numerous attempts to run its establishment in a more profitable form. An increase in the number of guests, and a reduction of standards of accommodation, were two items in a range of 'solutions' to the problem of the elderly. Indeed, the struggle to reduce costs, as we shall see below, is the major theme in postwar social policy towards the elderly.

SOCIAL WELFARE AND THE ELDERLY

In an earlier volume in this series, Gough characterised the welfare state as *'the use of state power to modify the reproduction of labour power and to maintain the non-working population in capitalist societies'* (1979, pp. 44–5). Gough argues that if we accept that all societies contain non-working individuals, it follows that they all must develop mechanisms for transferring part of the social product from the direct producers to these groups. However, the manner in which this transfer takes place and the range of goods and services provided raises complex issues. In the case of some services, financial investment by society may be regarded as having dual benefits. Thus, as McIntyre (1977) points out, education may be viewed as enhancing both individual self-development and as a form of investment in human capital. Similarly, services for mothers and young children may be seen as beneficial in terms of individual health and happiness and as a medium for assisting the productive or fighting capacity of the next generation. Provision for the elderly, however, does not have these 'dual pay-offs': 'not only may it be viewed as having no positive investment functions, it may also be seen as producing negative returns on investment by keeping persons alive and consuming resources even longer than they would have done without that care' (MacIntyre, 1977, p. 45).

Moreover, expenditure on the elderly may be seen as depriving other groups of support. Beveridge, as we saw earlier, counselled against being 'lavish in old age' until other vital needs had been met, particularly those of the young. Thus the subsistence principle which the Beveridge Report introduced gave no allowance — even in retirement — for presents, entertainment, travel, beer, postage stamps, newspapers, radio or tobacco. Despite this frugality, Harris (1977), in her biography of Beveridge, reported the concern in government circles with his initial proposals for old-age pensions. Lionel Robbins, in the Economic Section of the War Cabinet Office, was

> apprehensive that the proposals as they stood would require a level of taxation unacceptable in peacetime and might seriously hamper post-war investment. He was particularly alarmed by the projected expenditure on pensions which might preclude expenditure on other more important social objectives, such as technical education, relief of child poverty and post-war reconstruction.
>
> (Cited in Harris, 1977, p. 409)

As a result of such pressure, Beveridge modified his proposals, suggesting instead that subsistence-level pensions should be introduced by stages over a period of sixteen years. In fact, in the resulting legislation, no commitment to achieve this subsistence level was made. Instead of progressing towards subsistence, the real value of the contributory pension in the early 1950s was considerably lower than it had been when the universal system was first introduced in 1946.

The fate of the Beveridge proposals, combined with other items of legislation, introduces us to an important aspect as regards older people's experience of social welfare. Two conclusions can be reached from reviewing postwar legislation:

(a)   the failure, on numerous occasions, to implement original legislative proposals;

(b)   the refusal to acknowledge the failure of key items of
       legislation.

It may be argued that postwar social policy has been distinguished by conflict over the elderly's share of attention
and resources. Dissension has appeared at a political level
(e.g. in respect of the burden of pensions), at a medical
level (e.g. over the quality of treatment to be given to the
chronic as opposed to the acute sick), and at the level of
local government social services (e.g. how 'limited resources'
can be directed to the very old as well as the very young).
Out of this debate no agreement has yet to emerge on the
range of services and support required by elderly people.

This argument may appear unfair given the expansion in a
number of services for the elderly. In the case of the meals-
on-wheels service, for example, over 41 million meals were
served in 1977, of which 24½ million were served in people's
own homes. This is double the figure served ten years earlier,
and ten times the number served in 1962, when the Ministry
of Health urged the expansion of the service (Cypher, 1979).
The figures reflect the increase in social services expenditure
in the late 1960s and early 1970s. According to a recent *New
Society* survey overall expenditure was then rising by 12 per
cent a year in real terms; capital spending rose by more than
30 per cent in 1972—3 and 1973—4. These figures, however,
need to be set within the context of very low provision in the
1950s and early 1960s:

>   An enormous backlog of unmet need was known to exist.
>   And while the expanding social services began to clear the
>   backlog, they were at the same time taking on responsibil-
>   ity for the long-term social care of the elderly, chronic
>   sick and disabled from the NHS.
>   (*New Society*, 10 July 1980)

Even now, despite this expansion, only a minority of
elderly people receive domiciliary services. Only 3 per cent
receive meals at home, 9 per cent use the home-help service
and 11 per cent receive visits from chiropodists (Cypher,
1979). These services will need to be greatly expanded to

meet the needs of a growing population of very elderly people (the number of people aged 85 and over will increase by one-third between 1980 and 1990). Unfortunately, as we shall see below, public expenditure cuts are dealing a savage blow to precisely these services. The question to be asked is: how far is this a new trend and how far is it the continuation of a deeply rooted historical tradition?

SOCIAL REFORM AND THE ELDERLY

In the previous section the failure to introduce subsistence-level pensions was used to illustrate an argument about the relationship of older people to welfare legislation. Different aspects of this relationship are brought out if we examine the 1946 National Health Act and the 1948 National Assistance Act. Wicks and Hall (in Wicks, 1978) suggest that in both measures welfare for the elderly took a back seat. They argue:

> Despite the striking statement of the 1948 Act that from the appointed day 'The existing poor law shall cease to have effect', the early post-war reforms made little impact on social welfare provisions for the old. They meant little more than a re-ordering of organisational boundaries and responsibilities for existing services.
>
> (from Wicks, 1978, p. 120)

But the nature of the reforms proposed and the limited impact they made reveal much about the position of the elderly under capitalism.

In the 1948 Act there was little statutory provision for older people; what there was largely concerned the provision of residential accommodation. The underlying assumption was that the National Insurance Act and the National Health Act would provide for the financial and medical needs of older people. Beyond this it was regarded as the duty of the individual and his or her family (aided by voluntary agencies) to provide for old age, the exception being the minority who required 'care and attention not otherwise available to them' (Brown, 1972, p. 28).

The emphasis on residential provision is of considerable significance. Parker sees this as the continuation of a Poor Law tradition, and she contrasts this aspect of the legislation with the Children's Act passed in the same year:

> The concern to maintain and foster family life evident in the Children's Act was completely lacking in the National Assistance Act. The latter made no attempt to provide any sort of substitute family life for old people who could no longer be supported by their own relatives. Institutionalised provision was accepted without question.
>
> (Parker, 1965, p. 100)

The bias towards institutions was a dominant feature in the care of the mentally infirm elderly. Eleven years after the National Assistance Act, the Mental Health Act was encouraging local authorities to do more for this group. According to Bosanquet (1978) very few authorities responded to this plea. The reaction of some, however, was to start special homes. Very few considered day centres or social clubs for the mentally infirm elderly.

Despite the emphasis on institutions, progress on improving the quality of life of their inhabitants remained extremely slow. In 1948 the Ministry of Health supported the construction of more humane homes for older people. However, building was almost immediately delayed with constraints on capital investment and steel shortages. Reviewing the progress made in the 1950s, Towsend remarks:

> Few of the old institutions were closed. Short term plans for modernisation and conversion were held up because of shortage of funds and pressure on accommodation, but also because some Local Authorities were reluctant to spend money on buildings scheduled for eventual abandonment ... In 1949, of the 42,000 residents in local authority accommodation, about 39,000—40,000 were in Public Assistance Institutions. In 1960 the comparable figure was

35,000. The policy of replacing the old stock had not made much headway.

(Townsend, 1962, p. 35)

By 1953 the Ministry of Health was criticising local authorities for extravagance in the design of homes, and in 1955 a policy of building homes for up to sixty people was being recommended as more economical (Parker, 1965). With economy in mind the utility of second-hand furniture was also stressed, though it was felt also to be both 'congenial and more suitable to old people' (Brown, 1972, p. 38) Five years later, however, a concern for a more homely atmosphere in residential accommodation led to official acknowledgement that homes with sixty were too large. The atmosphere prevailing in many residential institutions was exhaustively surveyed in the fifties by Townsend. In *The Last Refuge* he detailed the squalor existing inside the old workhouse buildings and the 'grave deficiencies' apparent in many postwar homes. Townsend's report, with its haunting photographs of men and women sitting in huge dormitories (some without carpets and with only primitive decoration) is an appalling indictment of the limits to postwar reform. Townsend wrote with a vivid sense of shock of his own first visit to a former workhouse:

The first impression was grim and sombre. A high wall surrounded some tall Victorian buildings, and the entrance lay under a forbidding arch with a porter's lodge at one side. The asphalt yards were broken up by a few beds of flowers but there was no garden worthy of the name. Several hundred residents were housed in large rooms on three floors. Dormitories were overcrowded, with ten or twenty iron-framed beds close together, no floor covering and little furniture other than ramshackle lockers. The day-rooms were bleak and uninviting. In one of them sat forty men in high-backed Windsor chairs, staring straight ahead or down at the floor. They seemed oblivious of what was going on around them. The sun was shining outside but no one was looking that way. Some were seated in readiness at the bare tables even though the midday meal was not to be served for over an hour. Watery-eyed and feeble, they looked suspiciously at our troupe of observers and then returned to their self-imposed contemplation. They wore shapeless tweed suits and carpet slippers or boots. Several wore caps. Life seemed to have been drained from them, all but the dregs.

(Townsend, 1962, p. 4.)

Twenty years on, the following picture has been given of a residential home 'representative of hundreds up and down the country':

The building itself is modern and purpose-built and is centred in the middle of spacious and well-kept grounds with attractive flower beds. Strangely enough it looks nothing like a place where people live permanently in as normal a manner as possible. What we are looking at is a building which resembles a whole range of other public buildings and could almost just as equally be a school, a public library, or perhaps more appropriately a museum. No attempt has been made to design the building to look like housing accommodation, and although the grounds are attractive they are tended by staff from the local parks. Seats and paths are so sited that the people do not actually encroach onto the grass and flower beds.

(Clough, 1980, p. 29)

Inside the home, the author suggests there is an atmosphere bereft of dignity, one 'removing the last vestiges of personality from the residents':

Ask why each bedroom is not provided with a private bath and WC and you receive an incredulous stare and mutterings about the cost and inability to supervise the bathing. Apparently, whether they like it or not, each resident has to be accompanied by a member of staff when being bathed. The bedroom is pleasant and airy and nicely furnished with what is obviously a regulation issue. . .

You are soon assured that residents' own furniture would be too bulky, dirty or simply make the physical care of the resident too difficult. Nobody knows whether they would prefer to bring in some of their own furniture, or indeed have a small pet like a budgerigar in the bedroom, but in any case they are dirty and would take up too much staff time.

(Clough, 1980, pp. 29–30)

Limited options elsewhere compound the difficulties for older people.[2] The progress in building sheltered housing has been slow and we are some way from Townsend's target set in the *The Last Refuge*, of fifty per 1,000 elderly.[3] Such inconsistencies in official policies on residential care have been matched by those relating to domiciliary provision.

By the end of the 1950s a movement towards community care had appeared in government policy. Brown (1972) suggests that it had gradually become apparent that the welfare issues posed by old people went far beyond the tiny minority who required care and attention in homes. As a consequence, she argues, there was encouragement for a variety of domiciliary and welfare services, and a growing realisation of the importance of co-operation among official and voluntary bodies.

However, whilst the official line became one of de-institutionalisation and support for keeping older people in the community, assistance in the form of finance and legislation was limited. According to MacIntyre:

Under the permissive powers of the 1946 National Assistance Act all local authorities in England and Wales had introduced home help services, and by 1963, 75 per cent of cases attended were over 65. Local authorities pressed the central government for more home helps but were informed that inadequate finance precluded this. Chiropody services were not sanctioned until 1959, despite frequent appeals from local government; the provision of home meals was not sanctioned until 1962, and had to be introduced as a private member's bill. Section 13 of the 1968 Health Services and Public Health Act made home help services a statutory obligation, and empowered the provision of laundry facilities; it was not only considered long overdue by many local authority workers in the field but was immediately postponed.

(MacIntyre, 1977, p. 55)

Studies in the 1960s by Hunt (1970) and Harris (1968) were to demonstrate the considerable shortfall in meeting the need for home helps. A recent analysis by Bebbington (1979) suggests that, despite the considerable expansion in domiciliary services, the real gains are not as substantial as *per capita* growth might indicate. The greater isolation of older people, combined with increased incapacity within the elderly population, means that demand has far outreached the supply of services. Indeed, one interpretation of Bebbington's figures suggests that the proportion of the moderately and severely incapacitated elderly in the community who received the home-help service remained almost unchanged, at about 20 per cent between 1962 and 1976 (1979, p. 122).

In the mid-1970s, an increase in domiciliary and related services was urged to ease pressure on residential accommodation and on hospitals. In a consultative paper, *Priorities for Health and Personal Social Services in England*, the Department of Health and Social Security (1976) suggested a 6 per cent increase in yearly expenditure on home nursing (and health visiting), a 3 per cent a year increase in chiropody services, and a 2 per cent a year increase in home helps and meals on wheels.

The timing of the consultative paper was unfortunate, 1976 being the year of major cuts in public expenditure by the Labour government (in February, July and December). The possibility of expanding these services was immediately abandoned; indeed, as noted earlier, they have been among the most severely affected by expenditure cuts. However, before exploring the contemporary situation we must examine in more detail the foundations of postwar legislation.

THE NATIONAL HEALTH SERVICE

Along with the National Insurance Act (1946) and the National Assistance Act (1948), the founding of the National

Health Service was seen to herald a significant improvement in the lives of older people. Prior to the NHS, medical treatment of the elderly had suffered through the institutionalised distinction between the acute and chronic sick. Superintendents in the Poor Law infirmaries would often try to exclude the elderly and infirm (already rejected by the voluntary hospitals), preferring instead the prestige attached to treating the acute sick.

The elderly, sick or otherwise, had a strong chance of ending their lives in the workhouse, where, with the use of pauper nurses, standards of care were often appalling. Abel-Smith cites the following example from the Christchurch workhouse:

> A man, aged sixty, suffering from heart disease, was allowed to lie ill and groaning, cared for only by other inmates in the 'old men's ward' of the workhouse, without proper food and attention, from Saturday night to Monday morning. He was then carried on the porter's back to the infirmary, where he died almost immediately.
>
> (Abel-Smith, 1964, p. 210)

The distinction between the acute and chronic sick was consolidated with the transfer of the hospital functions of the Poor Law to the major local authorities. For older people this administrative change was to mean very little in terms of standards of medical care. The acute sick were concentrated in better buildings, making 'the best use of such ancillary services as were available'. Unfortunately, as Abel-Smith argues, the price of achieving these services was to make it less easy to provide proper nursing services for the chronic sick. Hospitals for the latter were

> primarily staffed by unqualified nurses, and a number of institutions lacked even enough qualified staff to provide adequate supervision. The number of unqualified nurses at work in the hospitals rose from 15,000 in 1933 to 21,000 in 1937. Faced with the apparently insoluble problem of obtaining enough registered nurses for the chronic sick hospitals, some local authorities started a

special course of training for nursing the chronic sick. Despite the opposition of the College of Nursing, a second grade of trained nurses was introduced.

(Abel-Smith, 1964, p. 375)

Hopes that the NHS would radically improve the treatment of the elderly were not fulfilled. Honigsbaum (1979) suggests that conditions actually worsened after 1948, with reactionary attitudes towards the chronic sick spreading from the voluntary sector to the hospital world as a whole. Consultants who worked in upgraded Poor Law hospitals acted no differently from their colleagues elsewhere:

all preferred 'interesting cases' and those, in their minds, meant the acutely ill.

The patients who had always suffered the most from this attitude were the aged, and their position, in some respect, even deteriorated after 1948. Under the old Poor Law (as well as the 1929 Local Government Act), they at least had the right to a bed if they could pass the means test imposed. No similar entitlement existed under the Health Service. Patients gained entry to hospital beds only if consultants accepted them, and few consultants, where the aged were concerned, felt so inclined. By 1953 the plight of the old had become serious.

(Honigsbaum, 1979, p. 309)

Documents such as the Boucher Report (1957) and *Sans Everything* (Robb, 1967) were to confirm the prejudice against the elderly within medical circles. Bosanquet sees the postwar period as a constant 'battle for the soul of the medical profession' (1978, p. 131). Despite the undoubted achievement of geriatricians such as Isaacs, Warren, Brocklehurst and Exton-Smith, the medical profession at large has been slow to accept the possibilities of rehabilitation of the elderly. As late as 1972 the Annual Report of the Hospital Advisory Service could report:

Unfortunately hostility to geriatric staff can be found at all levels in the hospital service and I am sorry to say that prejudice and lack of understanding can occur amongst the most eminent in a Teaching Hospital as well as in the most isolated rural group. For example, a Professor of a well known Teaching Hospital was heard to say that 'medical students should not be contaminated by contact with geriatric patients'. At another hospital the senior physician said 'geriatricians are undesirable'.

(Cited in Bosanquet, 1978, p. 131)

Such attitudes have flourished in a situation where the geriatric sector has often taken the lowest share of resources — whether for buildings, staff, equipment or research. Despite the regular issuing of circulars — from the 1950s onwards — insisting on the need to improve services for old people, changes have been restricted to the margin. Bosanquet (1978) concludes that the elderly have been provided with standards of treatment 'very much lower than those thought proper for other groups'. He argues:

Thus the elderly have been provided with a service which has been almost entirely set by society's view of what it thought it could afford, rather than one fitted to the elderly's particular needs. It has been a case of segregation rather than specialisation. Certain powerful myths and misconceptions have limited aspirations at all levels, and as a final irony the elderly are themselves blamed for blocking the service. A truly preventive and community-based health service for the elderly remains a pious aspiration — and a faint hope.

(Bosanquet, 1978, p. 151)

THE ECONOMIC CIRCUMSTANCES OF PENSIONERS

A major pillar of support for the elderly was the system of National Insurance introduced in 1946. Accompanying this legislation came optimism that the scourge of poverty among old people would finally be removed. After poverty, the key problems of old age were thought to be connected with the 'unwanted leisure' brought about by retirement. Thus most enquiries in the 1950s either concerned themselves with the psychological problems of retirement or the economic burden of pensions. There was little acknowledgement that poverty among pensioners was still widespread.

Doubts did still persist, however, among some government critics in this period. A group of trade unionists, advocating a plan for industrial pensions, began their pamphlet with the following statement:

> The plight of the retired worker is a national disgrace. Among all the many tasks that demand the attention of government at home, we give pride of place to proper pensions for the aged.
>
> Our trade union movement has achieved a reasonable and regular wage for those at work. But our fathers who fought for and won the great power which the movement holds today are left in shabby need. *For the aged, it is still the hungry thirties; for many still the dole.* Some depend upon their families for the modest comforts they have earned; others upon the kindness of friends and neighbours; not a few go lonely and frugal to the grave.
>
> (Fabian Society, 1956, p. 3)

With considerable foresight the pamphlet foresaw the possibility of 'new class distinctions' appearing in old age:

> We are deeply concerned at the prospects of inequality in old age being much greater than inequality in working life . . . On the basis of present pension plans about a third of the working population will retire with both a retirement pension and a pension from their work. The remaining two-thirds will have to exist on their retirement pension alone – or else suffer the humiliation of applying for national assistance.
>
> (Fabian Society, 1956, p. 7)

Material deprivation was reflected in public health reports and in dietary surveys in the 1950s. They indicated major deficiencies in the food intake of many older people. A survey in Stockport revealed that hardly more than half the

older people interviewed had a hot meal each day; an apprec-
iable number had no hot meal at all — this rising from 5 per
cent in social classes 1 and 2 to 11 per cent in social classes
4 and 5 (Fraser Brockington, 1965).

Barbara Wootton, writing in 1959, summarised a number
of studies suggesting problems of malnutrition among the
elderly:

> A study by two doctors showed that, in 1951–2, one in
> every thirty-six non-selected admissions to two medical
> blocks of a general hospital (which dealt mainly with the
> older age groups) suffered from malnutrition. Out of thirty-
> nine such cases, thirty-three were over sixty years of age,
> and in twenty-nine cases the lack of proper food was
> ascribed to poverty. 'Some seriously ill patients in advanced
> states of semi-starvation presented a typical appearance,
> identical with that seen among prisoners at the Belsen
> camp [Fuld and Robinson, 1953]'. Again in Sheffield a
> study of over 400 old people of all social classes, the
> results of which were published in 1955, found that as
> many as 20 per cent were in a state of poor nutrition, and
> that 'a substantial minority of the elderly were unable to
> pay for the necessities of life on a subsistence basis at the
> time of the survey' [Hobson and Pemberton, 1955].
>
> (Wootton, 1959, p. 78)

The nutrition problems of the elderly have continued up to
the present day. A recent DHSS report estimated malnutrition
at 7 per cent among its sample of the elderly (DHSS, 1980).

Peter Townsend's 1957 Bethnal Green study was one of
the first to highlight the severe drop in income experienced
upon retirement (a fall of over two thirds for the single and
widowed, and 50 per cent for a couple). In this study a third
of the respondents had a personal income below the National
Assistance Board's subsistence minimum and a quarter were
not receiving assistance but would have qualified for it had
they applied.

It was not until 1962, however, with the publication of
The Economic Circumstances of Old People by Cole and
Utting that a debate on poverty among older people really

began. The findings of the survey (conducted between 1959 and 1960) revealed a heavy reliance by the old on the state pension (much greater than had previously been thought), and the severe economic difficulties faced by single and widowed women. The response to this survey (the first to be carried out since the war) illustrates both the complacency and hostility which the issue of public pensions is capable of arousing. The Conservative government of the day urged that the document be 'treated with reserve', particularly since it was based on 'only 500 cases'.[4] The rejection of the survey's findings were highlighted in a parliamentary debate in 1962. Margaret Thatcher (Joint Parliamentary Secretary to the Minister of Pensions and National Insurance) suggested:[5]

> The question is often asked whether anyone can be expected to live on the retirement pension of 57s. 6d. or the National Assistance Scale of 53s 6d. The obvious answer is that no one is expected to because there are other resources available. Of the 5½ million pensioners today, many have private resources, or are members of occupational pension schemes and are receiving benefits from them. Also 1¼ million pensioners have earned increments to the basic pension by deferred retirement.
>
> (*Hansard*, vol. 655, cols 1161–1162, 1962)

Subsequent studies (including one by the Ministry of Pensions, 1966) were to question the existence or adequacy of these 'additional resources'. The 1965 survey by Townsend and Wedderburn stressed the minimal assets held by many older people. The Ministry's own survey of pensioner finances revealed the inadequacy (as well as the class bias) of occupational pensions. As regards the increment gained through deferred retirement, the average value in 1960 was 7s. 9d. and five years later 9s. 10d. – hardly figures which supported Thatcher's case. Moreover, at the time she was speaking the number of pensions awarded each year with an increment had gone into a significant decline (George, 1968, p. 160).

It is important to comprehend the intensity of the pensions debate. The Minister for Pensions, in a speech a few weeks after the debate, accused the Labour Party of returning 'to their old vomit of pensioneering' and complained about the clamour over pensioners, despite increases in the value and the level of the state pension, (*The Times*, 8 March 1962). Eventually, however, the government were to allow an enquiry into pensions, though it still doubted the likelihood of large numbers of older people living below the National Assistance Board scale rates. The results of this enquiry, combined with the follow-up study by Townsend and Wedderburn, were emphatic. The government study showed that 14 per cent of all retirement pensioners would have received national assistance had they applied for it, i.e. they were living below the offical poverty line (Ministry of Pensions, 1966). The Townsend and Wedderburn (1965) study found that for seven out of ten old people income from the state was their main source of income. The study also confirmed the important finding of Cole and Utting that single and widowed women had the lowest incomes of all elderly people. It also noted that the older you were, the lower your income was likely to be.

These studies were followed by numerous reports confirming the plight of older people both financially and in areas such as housing and access to social and community services. What is remarkable, however, is the huge time gap between acknowledgement of the severity of poverty in old age and the ultimate reform of pensions. The Labour Party took office in 1964, proclaiming its commitment to an urgent review of the whole social security structure. Nevertheless, it was not until 1969 that major changes towards earnings-related benefits were published. According to Kincaid:

The delays and postponements which characterised the pensions policy of the [1964–1970] Labour Government were aptly summarised by Douglas Houghton, the Minister originally responsible for the 'Major Review'. In 1966 he told the Commons that: 'We are now engaged in an urgent study of the whole problem and have been for a long time.'
(Kincaid, 1973, pp. 127–8)

Kincaid sees this vacillation as representative of a switch in ideology within the Labour leadership, with a retreat from the politics of social equality and wealth redistribution. Thus he argues, that when compared with earlier schemes, the eventual proposals for reform discriminated against the lower paid in favour of the higher income groups. Where income redistribution was effected it appeared mainly at the expense of the better-paid section of the working class and the lower-paid section of the middle class. As Kincaid remarks, 'The rich would escape lightly' (1973, p. 179).

The subsequent defeat of Labour in 1970 led to their proposals on pensions being abandoned by the new Tory government (although the Tories' own proposals bore many similarities to Labour's plan). Eventually, after another change of government, reform came in the shape of the 1975 Social Security Act. Ten years after the publication of the first major postwar surveys on the extent of poverty in old age, the reform of pensions had finally arrived. In essence the new legislation was a compromise between Labour and Conserative proposals. According to David Piachaud:

> While the new pension scheme may have been the best available compromise, it is not about to cause a sudden transformation in the circumstances of those retiring. It will be well into the next century before most pensioner couples have a pension of half average earnings. The White Paper estimated that the new scheme would raise the pensioner's share of total personal consumption from 10 per cent to 13 per cent over the next 40 years; this may be compared with the shift of 1½ per cent of gross domestic product to social security over Labour's five years. The pension prospects of women are certainly better under the new scheme than under previous proposals and the prospects for widows who will be able to inherit their husbands' pension rights are markedly improved. But those already retired gain nothing from the new scheme. (Although the White Paper stated, 'With the introduction of the new scheme, the position of existing pensioners will be further reviewed in the light of the development of the economy', nothing was done.)
>
> (Piachaud, 1980, p. 178)

To say nothing had been done needs qualification. In the case of the uprating of pensions, for example, a significant change was to occur. The DHSS (1978) discussion paper *A Happier Old Age* proclaimed that with the index-linking of the state pension to prices or earnings (whichever rose faster) pensioners were assured of a 'continuing real increase . . . in the value of [their] pension' (1978, p. 21). This commitment was abandoned two years later by a new Tory government and the real value of the state pension, contrary to the intentions of the Discussion Paper, has declined. Townsend's study *Poverty in the United Kingdom* (1979) suggests a bleakness in the lives of many non-institutionalised elderly (reminiscent of his earlier account of the institutionalised elderly). Here are two examples from Townsend's work:

> Mrs Hooton is a married woman of 65 who was separated from her husband four years ago and is living alone in a council flat in an old Victorian house in Edinburgh. She is a cheerful plump person who was very diffident about the interview, which was twice interrupted by neighbours (both elderly) dropping in on their way home. The house is sandwiched between a car park created after the demolition of adjoining property and a busy road. . . She did not have a summer holiday and seldom goes out. She has not had an evening out in the past fortnight. She has one cooked meal each day. . . [and] a pint of milk each day. At Christmas she spent nothing on presents. 'I would have liked to, but everything was too dear.' In winter she goes to bed at 8.30 p.m. While she thinks her situation has become worse in recent years, and is worse than it has ever been, she still considers she is as well off as others in the neighbourhood, and is 'never' poor.
>
> (Townsend, 1979, pp. 310, 311)

> Mrs Tillson, 72, has lived in a one-roomed council flat on the ground floor of a block of flats in Leicester for the last two years. The flat does not have a yard or garden, but has good facilities (though it is not centrally heated). Until she was in her mid sixties, she worked as a cleaner in a launderette. Her husband, a lorry driver, died fourteen years ago. She is hard of hearing (but has no aid), and has

severe arthritis and therefore difficulty in moving about. She can only mount stairs with great difficulty, and cannot carry a heavy shopping basket, for example. Most other personal and household tasks she can undertake only with difficulty. . . . Mrs Tillson finds it difficult to manage on her income and feels worse off than her relatives and worse off than previously in life. During the winter she had gone to bed early because she could not afford to burn electricity. 'I just manage to pay for the food, the TV rental and the coins for the electric fire. I've no money left for anything new for the home.' Poverty, for her, is 'having to count every penny all the time'.

(Townsend, 1979, p. 323)

PUBLIC EXPENDITURE CUTS AND THE ELDERLY

In its consultative document *Priorities for Health and Personal Social Services in England*, published in 1976, the DHSS reasserted the importance of keeping the elderly in their own homes for as long as possible. To assist this, it was argued, domiciliary services needed to be increased by substantial amounts (6 per cent in the case of home nursing; 3 per cent for chiropody services, etc.). The document argued:

Some of these suggested growth rates exceed the annual increase in the elderly population, and should therefore permit some improvement in the standard and scope of provision and help to keep to a minimum the use of residential accommodation which is expensive in both capital and staff. The level of provision of domiciliary services varies very considerably between localities. In some (including some localities where there is a high proportion of retired people) there is a very serious lack of these services. We suggest that in these localities an especially high priority should be given to building up domiciliary care.

(DHSS, 1976, p. 42)

Almost immediately after the report was produced, a succession of expenditure cuts was implemented by both Labour and Conservative administrations. These cuts have had a catastrophic effect on services to the elderly, and they represent a major departure from the tasks outlined in the *Priorities* document.[6] The most detailed information on the effect of the cuts emerges from the monitoring exercise of the Personal Social Services Council (1980),[7] and a survey by the weekly journal *New Society* (10 July 1980). An important conclusion of both is that while many authorities were reducing residential services, domiciliary and day-care facilities were simultaneously being undermined. Returns from the shire counties in the *New Society* survey suggested that as many as half might have reduced the level of their home-help service in 1979. The PSSC survey indicated that home helps and meals on wheels were favourite targets for economies. In the group of twenty local authorities from which the PSSC had the most detailed information, 80 per cent were planning to make savings in these areas. The effect of the cuts extend in numerous directions.

Many authorities report the closure of residential homes, and the abandonment of plans for building new ones; reductions in the level of staffing are increasingly common. Expenditure has also been curtailed in areas which directly affect the quality of life in residential homes. Westminster reported saving £1,000 by discontinuing the sweets and tobacco issue in its old people's homes. Other authorities report ending the provision of a subsidised hairdressing service or of newspapers and magazines; some save on food costs. The *New Society* survey found eight authorities who had begun to charge their poorest clients, supplementary benefits claimants, for their home helps. Similarly, services provided under the Chronically Sick and Disabled Persons Act are also a target for economies. The PSSC, for example, found two authorities who had ended free provision of televisions and radios to the old and handicapped; at least fifteen were considering cutting back on holiday homes. Since the PSSC survey was completed, the picture described in the report has almost certainly worsened. The implications of these cutbacks were analysed by the PSSC in the following way:

> Although the vast majority of older people live independently or with the support of family and friends, 'the elderly', and particularly very old and frail people living alone or without families are the major consumers of personal social services. At a time of *continued rapid rise in the numbers of very old, frail people at risk*, evidence from local authorities and voluntary organisations indicates that the consequences of the reductions may be an even greater shortfall in domiciliary provision, a poorer quality of life for those for whom residential care is unaviodable, resulting in less real choice of options, less chance of personal independence and a poorer quality of life for many old people and their families.
>
> The rapidly increasing numbers of very old people requires a substantial increase in services (after allowing for inflation and pay rises) merely to maintain services at their present level. *The long-term implications of the cumulative effects* or even a few years of actual decline in services may be to condemn present and even future generations of old and handicapped people and their families to unacceptably low levels of services.
>
> (PSSC, 1980, p. 17)

For those elderly people who have families we can see significant efforts on the part of daughters and sons to ensure that support is maintained. Contrary to popular belief, there is little evidence that the welfare state has undermined the commitment of the family towards its older members. Unfortunately, it is much more likely that the present round of cuts will place intolerable strain on daughters and sons attempting to care for elderly parents. By cutting back on holiday provision and day-care schemes, essential means of support for a single daughter or working mother may be removed. In addition, for the large number of older people with no surviving kin, severe hardship may be caused through reductions in services such as meals on wheels and home helps. Placed in this context, the plea for greater family responsibility is rather hollow. However, from a political standpoint it reflects a continued debate regarding the place of the elderly within the social structure, and the scale of resources they should receive. In the final section of this chapter we shall trace the historical roots to this debate.

CONCLUDING COMMENTS: OLD AGE AND SOCIAL POLICY

In the previous section we documented briefly the extent of expenditure cuts arising from the present economic recession. Important though the effects of these are, they must be set within a tradition whereby resources to the elderly are consistently reduced or withheld. Thus, although the new social policy emphasises the goal of family responsibility and individual self-help, this is not a novel theme in British social policy (it is, of course, rooted in a Poor Law tradition). Moroney (1976), and more recently Nissel (1980), have noted that elderly people have been much more likely to receive state help if living alone, or with a wife or husband, than if they were with relatives (particularly children). In the latter case, services have often been withheld on the assumption that the family will provide the necessary care. Alternatively, even when families cannot or will not provide care, services have been refused on the basis that they *should* do so.

In the early postwar period the rejuvenation of residential services was undermined through lack of financial support. Subsequently, community care was to become a major theme in government policy, only to experience a similar fate to institutional reform.

The absence of any sustained commitment towards the elderly is reflected at all levels of state policy. Townsend, writing in *The Last Refuge*, complained that

No serious attempt has been made by the Labour or Conservative Governments since the war to collect the necessary information or to review developments in policy. Between 1951 and 1961 the population of pensionable age living in Great Britain increased by 13 per cent from over

6½ to 7½ millions; if we look more closely at the oldest among them we find that in this same period the numbers aged 75 and over increased by 23 per cent and the numbers aged 80 and over by 35 per cent. Apart from some fleeting references in both the Guillebaud and Phillips reports, no government committee or commission has examined since the war the problems of the care of the aged.

(Townsend, 1962, p. 394)

In 1965 Towsend and Wedderburn complained that the government had made no special survey of the income and expenditure of old people 'despite the extensive debate on pension policy which [had] been going on' (1965, p. 76). (The government of the day eventually conceded an enquiry). Brown's description of Ministry of Health policy toward the elderly in the 1950s and 1960s seems to have more widespread relevance: 'The general impression is that the Ministry operated primarily as a restraining factor rather than a promoter of new ideas and moreover one which confined authorities in their endeavours as well as limiting them in their expenditure' (1972, p. 272).

More recently, the publication of a White Paper on the elderly has been postponed a number of times, and in the early 1980s' regime of expenditure cuts it does seem unlikely that a coherent framework of support will emerge. The conclusions drawn from a survey by *New Society* are particularly depressing:

Our public services are grossly unprepared for the enormous population explosion among the old, and more especially the very old. . . [Together with one parent families] they will impose a huge strain on [local authority social services] . . . and they are going to do so at a time when the ability of the population at large to provide informal care will be greatly impaired by unemployment and other public expenditure cuts.

(*New Society*, 10 July, 1980, p. 62)

The lack of preparation for the 'population explosion', however, has a more fundamental reason than the immediate crisis facing the economy. Throughout the postwar period numerous surveys, books and reports have warned about the 'age explosion'. While they may have disagreed about the means of tackling the problem, there has been unanimity about its existence and potential seriousness. The fact that the official response has been so derisory merits explanation. The most obvious reason has been indicated earlier in this book. In essence, the dilemma for the state has been the level of resources to allocate to the non-working/non-productive sector of the population. The tenor of the debate in the post-war period was set by the 1949 Royal Commission on Population, and its concern with the increasing level of consumption by the old and their corresponding decline in productivity. This theme was to be echoed in a number of publications in the 1950s. Writing in 1952 three Conservative MPs expressed concern that in twenty-five years' time 'Every man and woman at work [would] be devoting more than 12 hours a week to producing goods and services for consumption by old people who have retired from work' (Thompson et al., 1952, pp. 7–8). They went on to note the 'terrifyingly high' cost of pensions, and the conflicts which were likely to arise in the allocation of scarce resources:

> Should we build homes, hostels and hospitals for old people, or should the resources go into houses for young families and schools for their children? Should we raise pensions and National Assistance Benefits, or increase Family Allowances and expenditure on education?
> (Thompson et al., 1952, p. 10)

Nearly twenty years later, the Labour government's White Paper *National Superannuation and National Insurance* still echoes this concern with the elderly's level of consumption:

> At present, pensioners account for 10% of total personal consumption, and the rest of the population for 90%. The projected increase in the living standards of pensioners might raise this share of personal consumption to about 12% by the turn of the century, thus reducing the share available to the rest of the population by about 2% of the

total. The reduction in the share of personal consumption going to the working population represents the real costs of the real scheme, but it will come about only gradually over a period of upwards of thirty years

(Cited in Kincaid, 1973, p. 141)

So the obsession with consumption and productivity is a consistent one, and there seems little doubt that it will continue to exercise the minds of policy-makers, independently of a resolution of the present economic crisis. The need for the state to have a healthy work-force is one matter, whether it needs to have a healthy population of elders is quite another. The necessity of the former has been a major impulse in the creation of social policy. By comparison, the desirability of the latter has had only marginal influence. For the elderly the implications of this must be a greater reliance on their own organisations to challenge economic and social policies. Before examining these, I shall first look at the response made by professionals to the advent of an ageing population.

7

Care and Control of the Elderly

In previous chapters of this book I have sketched a framework for understanding attitudes towards old age. Attention has focused on the way in which state policies have often emphasised the 'burden' and 'uselessness' of older people. Official perspectives on retirement have rarely encouraged a positive view of this stage in the life-cycle, the condition of the economy at any one point influencing the acceptability of withdrawal from full-time employment. This environment had less destructive force when older people were a relatively insignificant part of the population. Now, however, with nearly one-fifth of the population aged 60-plus, state policies towards the old carry far greater impact.

In this chapter I shall examine the experiences and attitudes towards the elderly of groups in the health and social services. I have chosen the examples of social work and medicine because the responses made by workers in these areas reveal a considerable amount about attitudes towards the elderly. Moreover, the decisions taken by doctors and social workers about the management of resources have important implications for a range of other occupational groups (social work assistants, nurses, home helps, health visitors, etc.).

SOCIAL WORK RESPONSES TO THE ELDERLY

The elderly, particularly the very elderly, represents one of the largest groups in the work-load of social service teams.[1] In a study by the National Institute of Social Work of 2,400 referrals to a social services department area office, over 20 per cent of all referrals were from the 75-plus age group (this group represents only 5 per cent of the general population). The same study estimated that the area team was 'in touch' with one-eighth of the area's population aged 65 and over, and one-fifth of the over-75s. The team was in contact with around 30 per cent of those 65-plus who were appreciably handicapped (cited in Age Concern, 1981).

This degree of activity must inevitably increase given the projected rise in the population most seriously at risk, i.e. those in the 80-plus age category. However, according to recent research on the attitudes of social workers, antipathy is often expressed towards working with the elderly. Numerous studies of social work practice appear to confirm a view of the elderly as a low-status group, whose demands for aids and meals-on-wheels can be consigned to the responsibility of unqualified staff and volunteers. The reasons for such views have been attributed to various factors: the difficulty for social workers to identify any positive features in the lives of elderly clients; the guilt workers may feel about being unable to supply adequate resources; and finally, problems of communicating effectively with older people (Brearley, 1975).

The difficulty with all these points is that they could be applied with equal conviction to the majority of other groups with whom social workers are involved, groups which apparently receive far greater attention and which are more popular with social workers than elderly people. Much more convincing, I would argue, are a range of structural, ideological and organisational factors which reduce the priority of work with older people.

At a structural level, such work is 'unpopular' because of the tension between the relatively undeveloped state of social legislation, and social, demographic and economic changes. Of key significance is the contradiction between, on the one hand, demographic factors (the increase in the elderly population), labour-market trends (the movement towards earlier retirement), and, on the other hand, the pressure upon both formal and informal sources of support. For the present generation of retirees (particularly those from the working class) the extension of time spent on retirement has increased the reliance on the state retirement pension. The Tory government under Thatcher, however, reduced the value of the pension by severing its link with wages. Moreover, it is helping to promote divisions between pensioners and wage-earners by making increases in pensions and related benefits contingent upon increases in productivity.

In respect of informal support many older people are childless (30 per cent in the recent study by Abrams, 1978), and may have no relatives upon whom they can rely in times of emergency. In addition, the children of many elderly people are themselves beyond pensionable age and their own health and economic resources may be insufficient to meet the needs of an elderly relative. Finally, as we saw in Chapter 6, the crisis in public expenditure has forced major inroads into the availability of domiciliary and social services. Facilities which can assist older people to remain in the community — day centres, holiday homes, sheltered housing — are under severe pressure to increase charges to very high levels or close altogether.

The various conflicts outlined above will bring significant tensions to the lives of social workers. Given that social legislation (inadequate though it is) is weighted heavily towards children and families, social work activity with older people must inevitably be restricted. However, it is possible to 'resolve' the tension between an ageing population on the one hand, and the absence of social legislation on the other, through important ideological and organisational factors.

SOCIAL WORK PRACTICE: HISTORY, IDEOLOGY AND POLITICAL ORGANISATION

It is important to remember that during the period in which modern social work first emerged — the late nineteenth century — the number of people aged 60 and over were a relatively insignificant proportion of the population. Moreover, it was only during this period that the category 'old age' came to be singled out as meriting particular attention within the field of social policy. The liberalisation of workhouse policies towards the elderly did not occur, for example, until the end of the nineteenth century. This historical point, combined with the greater concern of the state with the condition of children and younger workers, meant that from its inception, social work attached marginal significance to work with the elderly. These trends were to continue, however, during the period of expansion in social services during the mid-1960s to the mid-1970s. While the priority of the state continued to be with children and the family, other factors emerged to reduce the popularity of work with the elderly, and I shall now consider these.

1. *The academic environment*

The period of social work expansion failed to stimulate research about policies and services for the elderly. In spite of the enormously influential work of Townsend in the 1950s and 1960s, no radical school of social gerontology emerged to provide critical perspectives on older people in the welfare state. Although in the USA gerontology emerged as a major field of study, few of the texts and articles produced fell into the hands of British undergraduates. Studies such as *Why Survive? Being Old in America* (Butler, 1975) found no British equivalent in terms of ability to provoke and influence radical thought. What is striking about the period of the 1970s is that the largest single group in poverty, and one of the major consumers of psychiatric and social services, was virtually bypassed in the radical theories, texts and organisations which were confronting British social work methods.

The limited development of gerontology was not helped by the influence on social work of anti-psychiatry and the sociology of deviance, both of which focused on the problems of children and young adults. These two areas provided an important contribution to social work courses, challenging traditional approaches to crime and mental illness. Their popularity, however, may have overshadowed the possibilities of work with older people. Anti-psychiatry directed much of its attention on the oppression of children within the family. According to Cooper:

The family specialises in the formation of roles for its members rather than laying down conditions for the free assumption of identity. I do not mean identity in the congealed essentialist sense but rather a freely changing, wondering, but highly active sense of who one is. Characteristically in a family a child is indoctrinated with the desired desire to become a certain sort of son or daughter (then husband, wife, father, mother) with a totally enjoined, minutely prescribed 'freedom' to move within the narrow interstices of a . . .relationship.

(Cooper, 1971, p. 25)

This focus on oppression within the family was, however, rarely treated — particularly by popularisers of anti-psychiatry — in a dialectical sense, i.e. that the father/mother/grandfather/grandmother, themselves both experienced oppression and felt a desire for liberation.

The concern of anti-psychiatry with the young is mirrored in the activities of sociologists of deviance. Studies on adolescent theft, drug-taking, experiences in school and at work were recognised as some of the most stimulating sociological work produced in the 1960s and 1970s.[2] By contrast, work on the elderly appeared pedestrian both in methodology and political content. A generation of students were introduced to problems of ageing via texts which — Townsend apart — ignored the major political and cultural issues being raised by deviancy theorists. Indeed, the field of ageing became identified as the one area where issues connected with political and class inequality could be safely avoided. Hence the appeal of work with the elderly to those seeking a rest from the ideological squabbles developing in other social work areas. Conversely, for those seeking radical therapies or political change, involvement with older people was judged to constitute a form of professional or political suicide.

2. *Organisational factors*

These ideological factors were buttressed by problems of organisation. The period when social services were expanding witnessed some intense lobbying from groups such as MIND, SHELTER and the CPAG. Imaginative reporting, combined with a more aggressive style of campaigning, gave a radical image to work in areas such as housing, youth work and family poverty. Organisations concerned with the elderly, however, took much longer to develop a more dynamic approach, failing to exploit the greater general political interest developing among groups of social workers.

SOCIAL WORK PERSPECTIVES AND THE ELDERLY

The influence of the factors discussed in this chapter are reflected in many of the texts and articles on social work and the elderly. Traditional casework methods are still central in most of these studies; alternative approaches are either ignored or treated as irrelevant to the problems of older people. Many of the arguments presented, even in recent studies, seem embedded in a former social work age: a period which still seems to be flourishing in the case of the elderly. Gray, for example, in a study on the mentally infirm elderly, suggests that 'The approach to agitated old people is very similar to that of a loving and imaginative mother to an overwrought child. She patiently presents pleasing and soothing alternatives to activities which she cannot condone' (in Gray and Isaacs, 1979, p. 110). And, summarising her thoughts on communicating with old people, she writes:

> Old people can be communicated with orally, by letter, or by non-verbal means. Due consideration should be paid when speaking with an old person to a possible deterioraton in sight, or hearing, or a decline in altertness and concentration, If the elderly person is agitated or deluded she may sometimes be calmed by talking about something pleasant in her past life. It is better to distract her from an irrational plan than to oppose it. Show interest, patience and warmth of response.
> (in Gray and Isaacs, 1979, pp. 110–11)

Contributions on what social work can achieve with the elderly are often depressingly narrow in scope and emphasis. Rowlings, in her study *Social Work with Elderly People* (1981), gives an example of support by a social worker to a woman facing transfer to a long-term hospital ward. In this case study the patient had not been informed directly by her doctor, even though the decision had almost certainly been made in her hearing. On the same day, the patient called the social worker over and

> She got hold of my hand and started to cry, saying 'They're moving me... I've been knowing it would come and then today the doctor didn't say good morning to me so I knew the time had come. They're moving me — well, at least I'll stop there till I die, shant' I?'

The social worker continued:

> I said, 'Yes, I know they're moving you, but you know we don't have an alternative, don't you, these wards are not for people who need a lot of care'... And when she said about being there till she died, I didn't say it to her but it looks like it to me, too, though a change of environment has been known to work wonders and physically, she could walk, she's just given up. And so I said, 'Well, it doesn't always follow, I know this is what it looks like now, but if perhaps you could get yourself walking again.' And I suppose I spent about an hour talking about the new ward and why she had to go there and just holding her... and it seemed that eventually some of Mrs Randall's distress and apprehension had diminished. When the social worker left, Mrs Randall had apparently been able to talk about the move with fewer expressions of despair and hopelessness — 'Oh, I shall be all right' she had said with some determination.
>
> (Rowlings, 1981, p. 59)

In her commentary on this event Rowlings places the main emphasis on the value of the brief period which the social worker could spend with the patient. The broader issue about the attitudes of doctors, other staff members and the role of institutional care itself is completely ignored. The possibility of the social worker challenging the practice of the institution is never raised. Moreover, there is a clear assumption that the social worker must accept that there is 'no alternative' to transfer to a long-term ward; the role of the social worker is simply one of making this transfer as humane and comfortable as possible.

The passive role given to social workers is reflected in broader definitions of social work practice with the elderly. Here, for example, is Brearley outlining 'the basic social work task':

[it] is the establishment of a relationship with the elderly client and the client's relatives or others in the immediate social network. As far as the elderly person himself is concerned the social worker can help him to consider the realities of his current situation and discuss the available alternatives in the present. Beyond this it will be important to help him see an ongoing pattern in his life. Contentment in the present will depend on an acceptance that what has gone before has been relevant; in part it may also depend on seeing value in the future. In this context reminiscence may have a therapeutic value in itself.

(Brearley, 1975, p. 109)

To find meaning and satisfaction with one's past life is doubtless important. But can it be regarded as having equal priority with the current struggle of many elderly people for a decent income and adequate housing and heating? Such struggles are barely mentioned in recent social work studies on the elderly. These texts transform problems of class and gender into private experiences. Events which occur in ageing and retirement are identified as exclusively individual dilemmas, to be resolved primarily by individual casework. The class/sex dimension to growing old is thus ignored; indeed, these factors are seen as relatively insignificant in comparison with the physical and psychological changes accompanying old age. This perspective, I would argue, has led traditional social work theorising on the elderly into a blind alley, with the neglect of some distinctive features of social work practice with the elderly. To understand these we must reconsider the relevance of class for the period of retirement and old age.

WORKING-CLASS EXPERIENCES OF OLD AGE

Social work with the elderly, as with most forms of social work, is overwhelmingly concerned with working-class people. If we fail to acknowledge this, then a major dimension to growing old is difficult to appreciate. As we argued in Chapter 2, from a historical perspective, longevity has been enjoyed primarily by the ruling classes. Health, of course, remains a political phenomenon. If you are in social class 5 you are 2½ times more likely to die before you retire than if you are in social class 1. Even within retirement, class differences in mortality remain pervasive. However, it is undoubtedly the case that more working-class people are surviving into their seventies and eighties: this fact is of major significance for social work. I would argue that the increased chances of survival have placed enormous strains on working-class incomes, institutions and relationships. Thus, while middle- and upper-class people have resources of health and income to support a positive view of retirement, the working class has approached this period with considerable pessimism. This negative attitude must, however, be seen as a realistic appraisal of the crisis, whether in the short or long term, which retirement will eventually produce.

I would argue that the conditions of working-class life (low or non-existent occupational pensions, environmental hazards at work, poor housing conditions) will undermine even limited attempts at preparation for retirement. If we accept this class dimension, then one important conclusion follows: growing old – given the inequalities described – means that at some stage (and probably sooner rather than later) *the majority of working-class retirees will register a degree of distress warranting social work intervention*. Problems may arise through the failure to claim benefits, problems with fuel bills, difficulties with house repairs, or conflicts with a landlord; in addition, problems may arise through the interaction between the physical and social contexts of ageing.

The condition of hypothermia provides a good illustration of this interaction. For the very elderly who will become less active and less mobile over the years, the amount of heating required to maintain health and comfort will almost certainly need to be increased. Old people will also spend a proportionately greater amount on heating because of the time they spend indoors. This requirement for more fuel comes at a time when people are receiving less income. This situation is complicated by the poor housing conditions under which people live (older people tending to live in older properties, often lacking basic amenities) which may make the maintenance of effective heating both difficult and expensive.

The extent to which cold is experienced, because of these factors, by elderly people has been documented in a number of studies. A study of the heating conditions of 930 elderly people in eight London boroughs found 230 (24.7 per cent) said they were too cold during the day to live comfortably; 190 (20 per cent) said they were too cold to sleep comfortably during the night; finally, no less then 111 (11.9 per cent) said they were cold both day and night (Islington Task Force, 1972). Wicks's major study of hypothermia found that:

> In general many of the elderly live in cold conditions and the majority had living-room and bedroom temperatures below recommended levels. Thus 77% of the sample had morning living-room temperatures at or below 64.6% (i.e. 0.6° F below the Parker–Morris standard), and 55% were below 60.8° F (16°C) – the minimum temperature specified in the 1963 Offices, Shops and Railway Premises Act. Similarly, bedroom temperatures were very low. Eighty-four per cent of minimum bedroom temperatures were below 60.8° F (16°C) while 33% were below 50° F (10°C).
> (Wicks, 1978, pp. 158–9)

These findings have added significance when related to research which suggests that the individual's natural ability to detect changes in temperature deteriorates with age; people may not realise, therefore, that potentially dangerous falls in temperature are taking place. These physical changes, combined with the social context (low income, poor housing conditions, etc.), lead to approximately 700,000 people 'at risk' of hypothermia (Wicks, 1978, p. 159).

I would argue from this example (and there are many others) that the idea of resolving such a vast area of need by a system of individual referrals or additions to social security is totally false. Instead, I would put the case for a more radical approach to the problems of old age.

The social work response: some alternatives

I have sketched above some of the ways in which capitalism affects elderly people. What, however, can social workers do? First, I would suggest that they can play a valuable role in disentangling two different themes which occur in the individual's experience of growing older: on the one hand, there are the physical changes and losses which occur during later life; on the other hand, there are stereotypes about these changes, arising from society's view about what individuals are capable of achieving in retirement and old age. It is important that social workers — in their involvement with older people — attempt to loosen the connections between these two areas. To put this point in a more radical way: *we need to de-condition older people about their own limitations*. People enter retirement expecting to slow down, expecting their health to deteriorate fairly rapidly, and worst of all they enter retirement expecting 'nothing' (this is particularly true of the working class). These, of course, are views which society has done very little to discourage, precisely because it means fewer demands being made — by retired people at least — upon the public purse. Even if, as is clearly the case, social workers cannot produce additional resources, they should not, at the same time, collude with the low expectations of many older people. They should ceaselessly question those older people who view themselves as a burden, or who say that they have no right to a better chiropody service, additional home-help support, or access to sheltered housing. Older people should be helped as much as possible to determine for themselves a more radical programme of activities and social support. By working with the elderly in this way, a more constructive approach to the tensions arising from inadequate or non-existent social legislation may be developed.

Second, and following directly from the above argument, social workers should become more actively involved in setting up neighbourhood groups of elderly people. These should be encouraged to give direct expression to the range of needs which exist among older people in the community. It is likely, given the composition of the population over 60, that the majority of people in such groups would be women (many of whom will be living on their own). With this degree of homogeneity, valuable work could be achieved in trying to get such groups to identify collective solutions to their problems — for example, communes, skill/learning exchange groups. Efforts could also be made at developing links between networks of older and younger women, to plan joint campaigns and to identify common areas of interest.

Third, social workers have a major role to play in challenging the attitudes of other workers in the health and social services field. An enormous amount can be achieved in the very difficult environment of long-stay wards or residential homes. The introduction of oral history groups, art classes, creative writing and poetry and drama groups can bring significant changes. But members of staff may find it difficult to accept alterations in the environments of homes and hospital wards. Norman quotes findings from a 1979 DHSS study of 124 local authority, voluntary and private homes in the London area:

> only 18 per cent could be described as 'providing a home, in the true sense, for their residents', and at the other end of the scale, 15 per cent were categorised as 'institutional' and described as 'rigid', 'unrelaxed' and 'tense'. In very few of the homes was there any form of consultation with the residents about the way life was organised; most of them did not encourage residents to help with chores or do things for themselves; few had any written or published statements of tasks or objectives. In about one-third of the homes early morning tea was served at 6.00 am and in some residents were called even earlier. The last main meal was usually served before 5.00 p.m. and some homes required residents to be in bed by 7.30 p.m. Lack of privacy, compulsory surrender of pension books and the absence of opportunity to make choices and decisions were also commented upon in the report.
>
> (Norman, 1980, p. 39)

Norman's work (and the report quoted above) raises fundamental issues about rights and freedoms within homes and
institutions. I would suggest that social workers can play a
vital role in securing these rights. They need to work with
staff and patients and identify alternative methods of work
and more egalitarian forms of decision-making. Democratic
structures are essential at all phases of life, and this is no less
the case in people's final years. The tendency to treat older
people as incapable of running their personal lives can only
hasten their alienation from life, and must weaken their
resistance to illness and disability. However, it is important
to be realistic about the possibilities for achieving change
within residential homes. Staff shortages, poor working conditions and low pay have a demoralising effect, destroying
any commitment to change. None the less, these conditions
themselves reinforce the need to transform the power structure within homes and institutions. A coalition of staff/
patients/relatives/social workers could provide a powerful
force for securing resources. By accepting the divisions
between these groups, political ground is conceded, and the
chances of moving towards greater freedom for the hospital-
ised/institutionalised elderly are substantially reduced.

DOCTORS AND THE ELDERLY

Many of the points discussed in relation to social work also
have relevance to an analysis of medicine and the elderly. We
have already discussed some aspects of this in Chapter 6, in
particular the bias against the elderly in the development of
the National Health Service. However, given the important
role which medicine – in some form or another – still plays
in old age, a more detailed review of the issues is necessary.
Hospital inpatient statistics for 1977 show that 57 per cent
of patients in non-maternity beds were aged over 65; in
Britain every year nearly one and a half million 'spells' in
hospital will be by the elderly (COHSE, 1981). The average
number of GP consultations annually for the over-65s is nine,
as opposed to four a year for people aged 45–64 (Owen,
1977).

For the elderly, therefore, important issues are raised about the quality of services, doctor-patient relationships, methods of treatment, and so on. There are also more fundamental issues about power and control within the medical profession, and, in particular, attitudes towards geriatrics as a branch of medicine. As suggested in the previous chapter, geriatrics is still considered a low-prestige area. In 1976 'only three out of ten London teaching hospitals had geriatric beds in the main hospital. It has been calculated that 750 geriatricians are needed in this country, but in 1979 there were only 349' (COHSE, 1981, p. 19). Geriatric nursing also suffers from the prevailing view that the elderly are a low priority group.

The picture drawn here would appear to repeat many of the themes discussed in relation to social work. There are, however, some important differences which should be noted. While social work has had to respond to a situation where legislation is heavily biased towards children and families, the medical profession has been able to exercise greater control over the definition of what constitute prestigious areas of work. If we take, for example, the distribution of merit awards: in 1973 four-fifths of all chest surgeons and three-quarters of all heart surgeons had their salaries augmented by awards; in contrast, a quarter of all consultant specialists in geriatrics, mental health and anaesthetics received awards (Peroni, 1981). Moreover, if a historical view of the development of medicine is taken, inequality in the treatment between the acute and chronic sick (the elderly representing a significant group within the latter) has been heavily influenced by the medical profession (see Peroni, 1981; Honigsbaum, 1979).

It must also be said, however, that the limited resources which geriatrics attract reflects more basic considerations about the costs and benefits of medical investment in the elderly. In 1977 expenditure each year on beds occupied by geriatric patients was just over £5,000 in comparison with £20,000 a year spent on medical and surgical patients. As regards staffing, there is one medical staff member for every forty-eight geriatric beds, compared with an average of one per thirteen beds in English hospitals as a whole (Counter Information Services, 1980). The condition inside many geriatric hospitals continues to be appalling:

> In principle many of these hospitals have been condemned for the last twenty years — 60 per cent of them were built before 1918. Many have not been modernised, maintenance has been neglected and the staff demoralised by an attitude that tries to pretend that they are not there! During a debate in the House of Commons on the 27th October 1980, Renee Short said, 'I visited one of the ancient Poor Law hospitals that is now being used for geriatric patients. It made my heart sink. I have seen many such hospitals in different parts of the country. The working conditions, as well as the conditions for patients, are deplorable.
>
> (COHSE, 1981, p. 14)

It could well be argued that facilities are kept so bad as a means of discouraging 'high' levels of demand. However, there are a number of other ways in which the medical needs of the elderly are controlled. Probably the most disturbing of these concerns the over-prescribing of drugs.[3] It is estimated that 10 per cent of old people admitted to hospital are there as a direct result of drugs prescribed by their GP (cited in Age Concern, 1977). Leoroyd reviewed the case-notes of all patients aged 65—plus admitted to a medical and psychogeriatric unit. Of 236 such patients, thirty-seven who had been receiving psychoactive drugs before admission and whose behaviour was disturbed improved dramatically when the drugs were withdrawn (cited in *The Lancet*, 15 July 1972). Sharpe and Kay monitoring drug prescriptions in a London pharmacy, found that

> Hypnotics, sedatives, transquillisers and anti-depressant drugs were frequently prescribed. The abundance of such drugs is higher than one might anticipate from morbidity statistics, suggesting that a proportion of these drugs is prescribed for elderly people without clear pharmacological indication.
>
> (Sharpe and Kay, 1977, p. 36)

Such findings are confirmed by Klass (1975), who saw the

elderly as special targets for drug companies. The vulnerability of older people to faulty or over-prescribing is increased by a number of factors. Older people are more likely than other groups to live in areas containing a high proportion of elderly GPs. Doyal suggests that doctors 'learn very little clinical pharmacology at medical school, and older doctors in particular may have scant knowledge of modern therapeutics' (1979, p. 194). We can add to this the point that such doctors are unlikely to have received undergraduate training in geriatric medicine (Isaacs, 1980). Under these circumstances, it is perhaps not surprising that the Age Concern profile on health services and the elderly, reported:

> Diuretics are frequently over used in old people for treatment of oedema and heart failure and can result in shortages of potassium, sodium depletion, postural hypotension and faecal impaction. The drug practolol is no longer available for prescription by GPs, but before it became evident that it caused eye damage sometimes leading to blindness, and severe skin infections, it is likely that many elderly patients had been treated with this drug and had suffered such reactions, as it is a Beta Blocking agent dispensed for angina of effort and cardiovascular arrhythmias. Amongst the psychotropic drugs chlorpromazine (Largactil), whilst an effective tranquilliser, is frequently given in unnecessarily large dosages and may give rise to jaundice and features of Parkinsonism.
>
> (Age Concern, 1977, p.34)

These findings would give less concern if there were convincing evidence available about great enthusiasm for the problems of the elderly at a primary care level. Unfortunately, while there are a number of important projects being conducted (see Brocklehurst, 1978, and Isaacs, 1978, for a review of some of these), the main body of evidence gives little ground for optimism:

> To some extent the quality of the service from general practitioners will depend on how satisfactory GPs find their work with their elderly patients. The results of

surveys are not encouraging. A study reported in *Age and Ageing*... found that medical students were less interested in the care of elderly people at the end of their clinical training period than at the beginning. A further survey, undertaken by Williamson, found that only one GP in three was particularly interested in elderly patients or obtained any job satisfaction from this part of their work. As many GPs are in one or two-person practices this must mean that some elderly people are getting a quite inadequate service from their doctor, without the choice of an interested doctor in their particular practice.

(MIND, 1979, p. 47)

THE ELDERLY AND THE SOCIAL ORGANISATION OF
MEDICINE

From the findings discussed above three aspects of the organisation of medicine can be isolated which raise problems for the treatment of older people. First, the historical division between the acute and chronic sick has made medicine both unprepared and unwilling to respond to the needs of an ageing population. While money and occupational prestige are allocated in disproportionate amounts to the acute sector, elderly people are unlikely to get a fair deal. Second, the elderly also suffer from the bias in medicine 'away from environmental factors and in favour of the illness model' (Ingleby, 1976). Given that the elderly are affected by a number of important environmental factors (the loss of close friends and relations, deterioration in their physical environment, poverty, etc.), there may be close interaction between these disturbances and illness behaviour. This type of relationship has received only limited acknowledgement within medical practice. Third, older people have been deeply affected by the bureaucratisation which runs through the welfare state. In this context Wilson (1981) is surely right to argue that we do not want more of the same type of welfare, but new socialist forms of welfare organisation. The position of older people in the hospital sector illustrates in an extreme form the alienation which many individuals feel from 'their' welfare state. In 1973 *The Lancet* published an anonymous article consisting of the case notes of an 80-year-old woman. The patient had died after three months in an acute ward. In its commentary on the case, an editorial in *The Lancet* made the following observation:

> There is another aspect of need which speaks for itself in these case-notes. One cannot read this account without forming the impression that the bed rather than the patient was the important subject at issue. It is not explained why the patient was referred and admitted to an acute medical ward in the first place, nor is there any account of a proper physical examination, an interview with the relatives, or early consultation with the social worker. The patient's incontinence appears to have been associated with heavy continuous sedation, and there is no note of this having been withdrawn or of any other medical treatment before her death from bronchopneumonia and recurrent urinary infection.
>
> In some active psychogeriatric assessment units the crisis calling for the patient's admission would have been analysed socially, medically, and functionally. With the earliest family cooperation, a plan for the re-establishment of the patient at home with whatever local-authority services, community nursing, and day-hospital support required would have been formulated and pursued through regular case-conferences involving the social worker, remedial therapists, and nursing staff. Intermittent discharge might have been arranged in the first instance to demonstrate that the patient was at least as well at home as in the hospital ward. In the case described here the specialists concerned appear to have abandoned any hope of improvement or of supportive care in the community once the label 'psychogeriatric' was applied. The social work department was called in only as an afterthought, and activity was largely confined to the problem of warehousing the patient for the rest of her life.
>
> (*The Lancet*, 3 November 1973, p. 1012)

In conclusion, I have examined in this chapter a number of features of professional practice towards older people. Apart from some limited areas of innovation, the overall impression is one of stagnation and conservatism in day-to-day work. Older people appear trapped within models of ageing which emphasise the deterioration and loss of function accompanying old age. Such models are, however, at last being challenged, not least by older people themselves in their own political organisations. It is to an examination of these that we now turn.

8

Political Struggle and Organisation

INTRODUCTION

Birmingham. A gloomy, windy Saturday. Early Christmas shoppers mingle with the faithful heading for the Aston Villa football ground. At the Civic Hall in Digbeth the box-office is taking money for a wrestling match on Saturday night; at the same time, in a small ante-room there is a meeting to discuss the problems of Britain's pensioners. The turn-out is not very impressive. Twenty people have braved a massive downpour and a bus strike to attend the meeting. There must be many more who cannot come, the organisers insist, but who do not know anybody with transport to bring them (70 per cent of persons aged 65 or more live in a household without a car).

The two speakers (a trade unionist and a churchman) valiantly attempt to instil life into a room whose appearance bears the marks of numerous public expenditure cuts. After the speeches, instead of the usual flatness and apologetic clearing of throats, there is an intense debate stretching over two hours. The first speaker – a 71-year-old man – talks of his own fear of senility, and his worry about who will look after him given the present climate of cuts. A trade unionist is next to speak. He recalls with horror having found an old lady dead in a block of flats – an event which shocked and angered him. How many more people would have the same experience, he asked, unless services for the elderly were drastically improved. The third speaker was a woman and she spoke – predictably perhaps – of the difficulties to be faced after losing a husband. She loved him deeply but now feels some anger at her dependence on him. Facing up to living alone is difficult enough, but such dependence places an additional barrier — a type of conditioning from which it is difficult to break.

And so it went on. Everybody had their say, contributing their own — often highly personal — account of what it meant to experience old age. People spoke about the problems of caring for elderly patients in a hospital starved of resources; they talked of the difficulty of working and of looking after elderly relatives at the same time; and they talked of managing on the state pension, of coping with inflation, and maintaining the type of life-style patiently developed over the years.

Such anxieties are likely to deepen while public expenditure programmes continue to lag behind the growth in the number of elderly people. Furthermore, the increase in the number of early retirement schemes is now adding a new dimension to the question of facilities for the elderly. The demand is not just for hospitals, clinics, meals-on-wheels, but for a whole new range of social, educational and cultural programmes to service and support older age groups.

The question I shall explore in this chapter concerns the political repercussions of these changes.[1] The interaction between an ageing population and an economic recession will pose major problems for the state given its desire to reduce expenditure of all kinds. The possibility of raising the statutory retirement age has already been explored in a number of countries with ageing populations (e.g. West Germany, the USA); and the question of raising the retirement age for women has already been discussed in Britain.[2]

A more likely policy for Britain is the adoption of self-help/voluntary social work strategies to replace some of the work financed by central and local government (a theme developed in the government's White Paper on the elderly — *Growing Older*). Here the distinction between the 'young-old' (those aged 55—75) and the 'old-old' (those over 75) is likely to be used as an instrument of social policy, with the former under increasing moral pressure to take over some of the tasks involved with the care of the infirm and disabled.

As an additional strategy, the momentum of expenditure cuts is likely to lead to a tight control over the range of

resources the elderly can 'legitimately' demand. Older people
– already highly dependent on state facilities of all kinds –
will feel increasingly vulnerable in a climate of exhortation to
reduce spending on health and social services. Whether this
climate will lead to political quiescence or militancy is the
subject of this chapter. Three areas will be explored:

(1) What is the likelihood of greater political militancy
     amongst the elderly?
(2) What type of pensioners' organisations have emerged?
     What are their strengths and weaknesses?
(3) What are the prospects for political organisation among
     pensioners?

THE POLITICAL SOCIOLOGY OF AGEING

The question of organising pensioners has been largely
neglected by the Left in this country. Although in the 1960s
and 1970s groups such as the unemployed, housewives and
tenants' associations became identified as potential agents
for radical social change, pensioners were largely excluded
from this process of 'rediscovery'. This absence of interest
reflected views on the Left about the kind of political work
to which older people might be receptive. Kincaid (1973), for
example, argued that although pensioners contributed a large
bloc of the electorate, they were relatively ineffective politically. He went on to describe them as poorly organised, containing a high proportion of non-voters, and tending to vote
consistently and as a matter of habit for one party ticket.
Simone de Beauvoir (1972), in her major study of old age,
suggested that having been removed from playing any economic role in society, older people lacked both cohesion and
a means of challenging their inferior economic and social
position.

Although all or part of these statements could be applied
to a number of non-elderly groups (many of whom have been
a focus for activity by the Left), the attribute of old age
seems to have encouraged widespread resignation. As a
result, work with the elderly in the 1960s and 1970s remained the province of established voluntary organisations:

precisely the groups who have in many cases depoliticised the field of old age.

Fortunately, this process has begun to change with the gradual emergence or more radical groups of pensioners. In the USA the work of Maggie Kuhn and the Gray Panthers has been particularly valuable in developing a more positive view of the elderly. In Britain we have seen the consolidation **of links between the trade unions and militant groups of** pensioners, **an alliance which has been beneficial in local struggles against expenditure cuts.**

In addition to the above, the movement of older people has started to develop its own writings, speeches and pamphlets, urging those in later life to initiate a process of liberation. Writings by Kuhn (in Hessel, 1977) Elder (1977) and Newton (1980) illustrate a new and more critical understanding of experiences in old age. This approach challenges problems of poverty and social isolation. It seeks to involve in the struggle for liberation hitherto passive layers of older people, and to bring together militant elements in both the younger and older generations. Here, for example, is part of a statement of principles by the American Gray Panthers:

> We are against ageism that forces any age group to live roles that are defined purely on the basis of age. We view ageing as a total life process in which the individual develops from birth to death. Therefore, we are concerned about the needs of all age groups and ageism directed at any age group. We have a strong sense of militancy. Our concern is not only for education and services, but for effective non-violent action with an awareness of timing and urgency.
>
> (Quoted in Hess, 1976, p. 464)

Before exploring how such aims are being expressed in this country, we must first investigate the likelihood of a radical movement developing among older people.

OLD AGE: A RADICAL FUTURE?

Any political sociology of ageing must recognise and work

within obvious constraints on the behaviour of older people. At various points in this book I have documented problems of disability, low income and poor housing. Older people may also experience more general environmental problems, residing in inner-city areas experiencing deteriorating housing and community facilities. Material factors such as these may have an important influence on political behaviour. Poor health, for example, combined with low income, may make it difficult for older people regularly to attend meetings. Moreover, with only a minority of older people living in households possessing a car, the availability and cost of public transport may be crucial in affecting a person's level of political involvement.

The influence of these factors will be reinforced by cultural stereotypes of ageing. Older people, as already described, are usually presented as apathetic and indifferent to political issues: voting only according 'to habit'. Worse still, there is, it is often argued, an inherent conservatism accompanying old age, with people beyond 60 or 65 becoming disinterested in the world beyond their home and family.

We need to understand more fully some of the feelings and arguments involved in these views. It is a common theme on the Left that the working-class movement is fragmented, with men and women, employed and unemployed, working in different groups with different aims and ideologies. But this works both vertically (i.e. across the life-cycle), as well as horizontally (i.e. among groups of similar age and status). Although the latter has received considerable attention in the work of Rowbotham *et al.* (1980), the problem of vertical fragmentation has been largely ignored. However, benchmarks in later life such as retirement and widowhood may loosen an individual's involvement in political groups. An active trade unionist may — in retirement — find limited outlet for skills at advocacy and political organisation; a widow may find that her commitment over the years to her husband and family has left her isolated in the years when she is most in need of support. These are without doubt bitter experiences and they raise questions about how successfully older people may be incorporated into social and political life within the community.

Such experiences, however, must be set within the context of important changes now affecting the elderly population. In particular, there is the rise of the so-called 'young-old' (the 55—75-year-olds). This is an age group for whom access to a wide range of life-styles will become increasingly important (particularly in a context of earlier retirement). In an American study Neugarten has described this age group in the following way: 'As a group they are markedly different from the outmoded stereotypes of old age. Although they are relatively free from traditional social responsibilities of work and family, they are relatively healthy, relatively affluent, and they are politically active' (1974, p. 196). The suggestion here is that a more activist population of elders is emerging, one with greater resources to argue and mobilise for social change. Neugarten foresees a transformation in stereotypes of what it means to grow older. She looks ahead to the 1990s and the entry into the young-old category of people who were active in major political and cultural movements in their thirties and forties, and who challenged institutions over the question of women's rights, Vietnam and the power of multinational corporations. She writes:

These experiences and their attitudes, combined with their higher educational levels, will probably lead the future young-old to exert a potent influence upon government. Compared to the young-old of the 1970s, the young-old of the 1990s are likely to wield their influence through direct political action and to make demands of both the public and private sectors to bring the benefit structure in line with their raised expectations.

(Neugarten, 1974, p. 197)

However, it might still be argued that despite the rise of this more radical grouping, the conservatism associated with ageing is likely to remain influential. Continued support for this type of argument — particularly on the Left — is in many ways surprising. Among socialists, for example, there is a tradition of opposing statements which refer to the innate superiority or inferiority of particular social groups. Instead, there is an attempt to search for political and economic motives behind forms of inequality and subordination. For example, in explaining why housework is an exclusive domain of women, we reject explanations centred on personal choice or female attributes. Instead, we look to the benefits to the employer and the cost of socialised alternatives, the effect on work discipline — the unwaged housewife and her children reinforcing incentives for the male to 'work regularly and hard' (Wilson, 1977, p. 177) — and the emotional support provided within marriage, turning the worker 'from a militant into a responsible citizen' (ibid).

For elderly people, on the other hand, arguments based on personal attributes are given more substance. Traits accompanying ageing are seen to 'explain' older people's indifference to politics and new ideas. We see older people resistant to changes in morality, rejecting greater freedom in areas of personal and cultural expression.

These connections are made partly through personal experiences of reactionary views held by older people. We may find them both authoritarian and racist, constantly referring to a period when life for them was better and more secure. We see their views as evidence of how the process of ageing weakens people's ability to view their world in a critical way, forcing them into rejecting situations which may demand a re-evaluation of their past beliefs.

There are, however, alternative ways of viewing the apparent conservatism running through old age. We might ask why it is that past experiences become so important for the elderly. Is it simply through the physical and psychological side-effects of ageing? Or is it a consequence of insecurities in the individual's present life? If older people sometimes seem authoritarian and racist (although these characteristics are surely shared with other groups), might this not arise through the pressures associated with living on a low income, and a concomitant (albeit unjustified) belief that additional resources would be available if there were fewer claimants?

I would argue, in fact, that the 'conservatism' of the elderly is a complex phenomenon, and that in practice it may be difficult to distinguish between a move towards the political right and social practices which define the elderly as a conservative group. The complexity of these issues may be illustrated if the question of voting abstentions and voting patterns is examined. In the case of the former, it is often suggested that the elderly contain a disproportionate number of non-voters, an 'obvious' sign, it is argued, of their political apathy. On the latter, it is considered, as described above, that age plays an important role in the realignment of political views (Abrams and O'Brien, 1981).

Perpetual and occasional abstainers are found among a number of groups: women, the very young, and the very old. The 'problem' is not therefore confined to a particular age category. Moreover, much of the abstention by the very elderly must, in Blondel's (1966) words, be described as 'artificial', arising through sickness or invalidity.

How the elderly vote is a question which needs to be examined with some care. Is it the case, for example, that they vote out of habit for one particular party? In the most detailed examination of this issue so far available, Butler and Stokes (1971) found that it is duration of party support rather than age itself which strengthens party loyalty. They suggest that age does not add to the strength of a long-established support for a party; among those with a fickle voting record, the old were, if anything, more weakly attached to their current party than the young (Butler and Stokes, 1971, p. 80).

The same authors also question the extent to which a gradual move to the Right is characteristic of ageing. Thus, when examining the age profile of party support (in the period of the 1960s), Conservative strength tended to be weakest among those in early middle age, i.e. those born in the 1920s and just before. Electors younger than this tended actually to be a little more conservative than those who lay within the boundaries of early middle age:

This irregularity, although an embarrassment to any simple theory of conservatism increasing with age, can readily be reconciled with the concept that the conservation of established political tendencies is what increases with age. The profile of age support in the mid-1960s can be accounted for in terms of the impress of early political forces on the young and the preservation of these forces in the hardening allegiances of later years. We must ask not how old the elector is but when it was that he was young. Voters who were of early middle age in this period, among whom Conservative support is weakest, were too young to have voted before the Second World War but entered the electorate in the postwar Labour flood. Electors who were older than this came of age when Labour was far weaker; indeed, many reached maturity before the Labour Party could establish any serious claim to power. We would expect electors who were younger than the 1945 cohort to be most variable in their party support, since they were still, in the 1960s, in their impressionable years.

(Butler and Stokes, 1971, p. 83)

This generational model, however, may understate the fickleness of voting behaviour. Between 1945 and 1966 those below 30 years of age consistently favoured Labour, but by margins varying from 1 per cent to 28 per cent. In 1964 and 1974 the margin of support given to Labour by those under 35 also fluctuated. Although the elderly favoured the Conservatives at both these elections, the 1951 and 1959 elections saw a trend towards support for Labour (Alderman, 1978).

If we look at research on the general attitudes of older people, the evidence does not support a consistently conservative line on key social issues. In a summary of American research, Riley and Foner found that

Compared with younger generations, [the elderly] allied themselves sometimes more with the right and sometimes more with the left. Toward the pole perceived as conservative, people over 65 were less favorable — but among the middle class only — to government control in general, less tolerant of political and social nonconformity... But the elderly were more liberal on [some] issues. People sixty-five and over were more likely to feel that the government should help those [seeking] ...work, more favorable to public housing, and more supportive of publicly owned utilities.

(Cited in Baum and Baum, 1980, p. 79)

The most important lesson to be drawn from both British and American research is that old age does not force people into a fixed set of attitudes — social, political or otherwise. The burden of research — in Britain and America — suggests that differences within the age groups beyond 60 are just as marked (if not more so) in comparison with groups at earlier developmental stages (Puner, 1978).

We may conclude, therefore, that there are no direct obstacles arising from the process of ageing which will prevent old people emerging as a force for radical social change. However, the interwar and postwar history of pensioners' movements suggest that this is hardly a novel finding.

POLITICAL ORGANISATION AMONG THE ELDERLY

The roots of political organisation by older people can be traced to the 1930s. We saw in Chapter 3 the dilemmas posed for the elderly by the economic trap of inadequate or non-existent pensions and shrinking job opportunities. In the USA, for example, in the late 1930s less than 5 per cent of elderly Americans had pensions and 50 per cent were un-employed (Fischer, 1977). In Britain the old-age pension was generally regarded as barely adequate and pressure to combine improved pensions with early retirement was an important focus of political activity.

The Scottish Pensioners' Association and the National Federation of Old Age Pensions Association (both of which survive to this day) were established in 1939 following a number of meetings held in the late 1930s in various parts of the country to protest about the plight of elderly people. These meetings comprised mainly working class pensioners, intent on campaigning for improvements in the basic pension.

Despite the significance of these organisations, they arrived too late in Britain to affect materially the lives of pensioners in the 1930s. In the main, the problems faced by elderly people in this decade were revealed through the findings of social investigators; public marches or street vigils by pensioners had to wait a future period of depression.

In the USA, on the other hand, the 1930s saw the development of a vigorous pensioners' movement.[3] This was particularly the case in states such as California where migration had swelled the proportion of people 65 and over to twice the national average. The American historian Fischer (1977) has argued that the elderly were already organised in a way which facilitated some form of political action. Many, he writes, 'belonged to 'state societies' which brought together people from a single place of origin to share both their memories of the past and their fears for the future' (Fischer, 1977, p. 177). In the climate of a severe economic depression, these fears were to prove fertile ground for campaigners with schemes for old-age pensions. According to Fischer:

> In the warm sun of California, pension schemes grew in great abundance. By 1937 one observer counted more than eighty different plans in public discussion — ideas that reached all the way from a modest proposal to solve the problem of old age by distributing free fishing licences to the elderly, to schemes for full financial support of everyone over 65.
>
> (Fischer, 1977, p. 177)

One of the most widely supported schemes was the Townsend plan — advocated by a Dr Francis Townsend. Arguing that the depression was caused primarily by excess production, he suggested an old-age pension of 150 dollars a month for everyone over 60. The one condition for receiving the pension was that the money had to be spent as quickly as possible — thus helping to soak up any surplus stock. Support for the plan was immediate and swiftly took on the dimensions of a national crusade:

> In San Diego, for example, there were about 35,000 people sixty and over in a population of 180,000. By early 1935, 30,000 people in that city alone had become dues-paying Townsendites, and 105,000 had signed Towsend petitions. Thousands of clubs sprang up in every State — by 1936, there were 1200 in California alone.
>
> (Fischer, 1977, p. 181)

Although a national system of social security was introduced in 1935, it would be misleading to view this as a direct consequence of the activities of groups such as the Towsendites (indeed, Townsend's greatest popularity came, as Fischer points out, 'after the act, in reaction to its limitations' (1977, p. 183). Many of the organisations were beset by internal schisms and had limited impact at lobbying at a national level. Their importance, however, was to influence a climate of opinion in favour of old-age pensions. Additional support for a system of social security came through changes within industry and the economy. American capitalism, in the 1920s and 1930s, came to recognise the older worker as a marginal and expendable element within the labour force: a combination of changes in the technological environment (the spread of assembly-line methods of production) and the economic recession fostered debates on the 'inefficiency' of older workers and the best method for securing their removal from industry. In this climate, the old objections to pensions as 'destructive to the spirit of enterprise' (Fischer, 1977, p. 168) were rejected in favour of a limited scheme which would assist in 'preserving the traditional fabric of American capitalist and democratic institutions' (1977, p. 183).

AMERICAN OLD-AGE MOVEMENTS: THE POSTWAR
EXPERIENCE

Despite the undoubted weakness of the large-scale movement for old-age pensions, its existence serves to remind us of a history which is often ignored when discussing political work among older people. What, however, has been the postwar experience of such movements?

In the case of the USA two main trends can be identified. In the 1950s and 1960s we find the consolidation of a more influential – in national terms – old-age lobby, with the emergence of a number of groups capable of influencing the course of national legislation. The scale of organisation represents a significant break from the groups of the 1930s. While the latter often rose and fell with the changing fortunes of a single charismatic leader, the more recent organisations have, in the words of one analyst, 'found a resource base and bureaucratic structure necessary for smooth succession of leadership and increasing political access' (Pratt, 1976, p. 189). The three most important mass-membership organisations are the National Council of Senior Citizens (NCSC)— initially founded in the early 1960s to campaign for Medicare, but later expanded to cover the major issues facing older people; the National Retired Teachers' Association (NRTA) and the American Association of Retired Persons (AARP) — which, combined, function as one organisation; and the National Association of Retired Federal Employees (NARFE).[4]

These organisations now represent millions of older people and have undoubtedly achieved a high degree of penetration into national politics. The NCSC, to cite one example, played a significant role in the passage of Medicare (health insurance for older people) and played an important part in securing the 1972 Social Security Amendments. None the less, despite the scale of poverty and deprivation among older people in the USA (almost 16 per cent of those over 65 have incomes below the federal poverty line; a further 10 per cent are considered marginally poor, with incomes that are below 125 per cent of the federal poverty line), all the organisations listed above take a reformist stance on questions of economic and social policy. According to Binstock:

> The activities of the ageing organizations in national politics are hardly political or radical. They do articulate and support many demands favorable to the interests of elderly persons. But their efforts do not reflect a vigorous pursuit of major policies that could bring about substantial changes in the fundamental status of the aged in American society.
>
> (Binstock, 1974, pp. 206—7)

However, the other important, and more recent, postwar development is the radicalisation of sections of the elderly, one organisational expression of this being the rise of the Gray Panthers. Originally founded in 1970 by Maggie Kuhn, this movement had by the end of the decade reached a membership approaching 15,000, organised in a network of eighty-six groups spread across the country. The initial aim of the Gray Panthers was to combat one of the most obvious and widespread areas of age discrimination — mandatory retirement. However, the movement quickly established itself as a campaign against ageism as it affected all age groups. In an interview, Maggie Kuhn argued:

> Young people are penalized by ageism as much as the old. It is difficult for them to get jobs, it is difficult for them to make themselves heard and have their opinions respected. We now need a re-structuring of employment to avoid these sharp differentiations. We are against ageism which forces any age group into roles which are defined purely on the basis of chronological age.
> (Cited in Whitehouse, 1978, p. 8)

In 1973 the Gray Panthers joined forces with the Retired Professional Action Group, which had been organised as one of Ralph Nader's Public Citizen Groups. Both organisations worked on questions such as the rights of patients in nursing homes and the regulation and reform of private pension systems.[5]

One of the issues being investigated by Nader concerned the hearing aid industry. As a result of this work a report was compiled showing how many companies were defrauding people with hearing difficulties, particularly the elderly. The Gray Panthers adopted this report and recommended policies that could be adopted to correct the situation. As a result many states have enacted legislation in an attempt to control and provide guidelines for this industry (Gray Panthers, 1976).

The Gray Panthers have also been prominent critics of the standards of health care for older people, conducting seminars and workshops throughout the USA. There have also been protest confrontations and marches at meetings of the American Medical Association, as well as the presentation of reports to a senate sub-committee on the health of the elderly.

Conventions organised by the group have explored alternatives to compulsory retirement, new approaches to the health crisis, women and ageing, consciousness raising, new politics and life-styles.

Whether the rapid growth of the movement will be maintained in the 1980s – in conditions perhaps less favourable than the community-orientated politics of the late 1960s and 1970s – is uncertain. None the less, the development of such a movement indicates the capacity of older people to initiate campaigns challenging basic assumptions about their rights and needs. Moreover, the Gray Panthers are not alone in developing militant and radical alternatives. The 1970s were to see analogous developments in Britain.

THE POLITICS OF AGEING: THE BRITISH EXPERIENCE

In the postwar period four main currents can be identified in the British pensioners' movement.

(1) There has been the growth and consolidation of postwar organisations such as the National Federation of Old Age Pensions Association (NFOAPA).[6] Since its foundation in the late 1930s, the Federation has built a membership of around 250,000. It publishes a monthly paper *Pensioners' Voice*, which includes reports from local branches as well as political commentaries. The stated aim of the Federation is to obtain – for a single person – a pension equivalent to one-third of the gross male average earnings in industry (50 per cent for a married couple).

The Federation has, as we shall see, come under attack in recent years for lack of militancy. Critics argue that social activities have come to play a dominant role in the life of most branches, with political campaigns largely taking a back seat. Against this, one can point to the heterogeneity of Federation branches, with areas such as London often adopting a more militant approach. Despite criticisms, there seems little doubt that the organisation will continue to wield an important presence in old-age politics. Its rise since the 1930s has, however, been overshadowed by the growth of a number of other organisations seeking to represent and articulate the needs of pensioners.

(2) The National Old People's Welfare Council (now known as Age Concern) was established in 1940; the National

Corporation for the Care of Old People (recently renamed the Centre for Policy on Ageing) followed in 1947 and Help the Aged (formed under the umbrella of Voluntary & Christian Service) in 1962. These organisations have conducted major campaigns over issues such as low income, hypothermia, poor housing and loneliness among older people. They have also contributed to the expanding literature directed at pensioners: Age Concern's *Your Rights* handbook, and Help the Aged's *The Time of Your Life* retirement manual being two significant examples.

All of these organisations, however, have retained a neutral stance on major political and economic issues. Their political work has been mainly concerned with increasing access to the main political parties and Parliament itself (despite evidence that Ministers are often hostile to the old-age lobby).[7] The form in which lobbying is carried out — via conferences, seminars, research papers, etc. — tends to exclude broad sections of the elderly. Very rarely are attempts made to organise around demonstrations or on campaigns involving the elderly within local communities. However, the passivity and depoliticisation this encouraged were to be challenged by important developments in the early 1970s.

(3) The failure of postwar legislation in the areas of health and social security (see Chapter 6) created the conditions for political organisation among the elderly. In addition, the social and political environment of the 1960s and 1970s — the struggles over bad housing, unemployment, women's rights — provided a fresh education in the realities of power and political lobbying. These insights, combined with the elderly's own experiences of attempting to cope on the state retirement pension, were to generate militant action.

Inside the NFOAPA dissent was expressed by some individuals over the organisation's non-militant stance. Subsequently, a group of Federation members in Camden, London, were expelled and set up their own organisation, the Camden Pensioners and Trade Union Action Committee, in 1973.[8] Like the London Joint Committee of Pensioners and Trade Unions which had been formed in 1953 it was committed to fight for higher pensions and to work in liaison with the trade-union movement. These two organisations, along with the Scottish Pensioners' Association and a group from Merseyside met in London late in 1973 to form the British Pensioners Trade Union Action Association (BPTUAA).[9]

The growth of this organisation has been quite rapid and it now has fifty regions and branches. The London organisation (the Greater London Pensioners' Trade Union Action Association (GLPTUAA) is particularly well developed. As early as 1974 a charter was prepared demanding a pension — for a single person — of 50 per cent of gross male average earnings in industry (75 per cent for a married couple). In the same year a meeting was held with the Under-Secretary at the DHSS to protest about the level of the state retirement pension; towards the end of 1974 a lobby was organised at the Labour Party Conference. More recently, deteriorating public services have provoked militant action at a local level. To quote from two leaflets produced by branches of the BPTUAA:

ISLINGTON PENSIONERS BATTLE AGAINST THE CUTS

We are Islington's Newington Green Pensioners Action Group. The advice centre where we have held our meetings for years was closed in September so we found ourselves victims of council cuts and began to take more part in local campaigns.

We have been to several large demonstrations outside council meetings. There is an Islington Cuts Campaign involving people from hospitals, tenants associations, playgroups, etc. One of our members is the representative for pensioners. Torchlight vigils outside local hospitals and the Town Hall were organised one night. We wrote to the *Islington Gazette* when it quoted the council leader, Gerry Southgate, saying there would be no cuts in social services. We know there have been cuts already and more are coming. We are always on the look out for new members and hope more pensioners will want to join us as we realise the full impact of these cuts on our lives.

PENSIONERS FIGHT TO SAVE TOTTENHAM HOSPITAL

The senior citizens of Tottenham for Action have joined

the Harringay Campaign against Social Services Cuts, and pensioner Tom Tiffany is an active member of the cuts campaign committee. When the Prince of Wales hospital was suddenly closed by the Area Health Authority, pensioners joined the hospital doctors and nurses in re-opening the hospital. The casualty is now operating for the public.

The doctors and nurses are fully supported by the pickets of pensioners, NUPE members and local MPs.

An important aspect of the BPTUAA's work is its links with the trade unions, with affiliation being achieved both at regional and national levels. The TUC has organised two national conventions of pensioners' associations. The convention organised in November 1980 attracted 3,000 delegates and the meeting heard calls for pensioners to attend a Senior Citizens Day of Action (held in the spring of 1981) to protest against government public spending cuts. A further important development has been the formation (in May 1980) of the London Joint Council for Senior Citizens. The council comprises the London sections of the three main national pensioners' organisations: the Transport & General Retired Members' Association,[10] the Greater London Trade Union Action Association and the National Federation of Old Age Pension Associations.

Links with the trade unions have had practical benefits in the current crisis over welfare expenditure, pensioners being involved in struggles to prevent the closure of hospitals, homes for the elderly, charges for home helps, etc.

(4) Finally, an important strand to postwar activities has been various forms of community work with pensioners. Although work with older people has formed only a small component in the growth of interest in community work, a number of important projects have been developed: self-help social clubs, health education groups and various kinds of pressure groups are among the best-known examples.[11]

POLITICAL AND COMMUNITY WORK WITH PENSIONERS: SOME EXAMPLES

Before drawing some conclusions from this review, I shall

look at four case studies of work involving pensioners. In the first two I examine aspects of community work with the elderly; the third and fourth examples look at the work of the British Pensioners Trade Union Action Association.

Community work with the elderly: Cleator Moor

Based in Cleator Moor, a working-class town in West Cumbria, the Senior Citizens Action Group (SCAG) was formed in 1973.[12] The decision to start SCAG arose from discussions between a worker from the Cleator Moor Community Development Project and pensioners at a further education class. There was concern among the pensioners about what could be done to help older people get repairs done in their homes. The work of the group can be classified under two broad headings: 'pressure-group' activity and 'self-help' acivity.

Early on in its life SCAG moved beyond its initial brief of organising a small jobs service for people's homes, to work on a range of issues affecting pensioners in the area. Some of the activities carried out in the past include: campaigns on pedestrian safety, concessionary bus passes, provision of a chiropody service.

Self-help activity has — for reasons outlined below — been a more prominent feature of SCAG's work. The group has attempted to combat the loneliness and isolation of the housebound through the organisaton of a weekly social club. Although originally organised around the needs of those who would otherwise have little chance to get out of the house, other pensioners have also been encouraged to drop in. In their description of SCAG, Butcher *et al.* (1980) point out that the weekly socials have provided a springboard for a range of activities, for example a welfare rights course, coach outings, and the organisation of a food and household-goods club. This last venture started in 1975:

> A small group of SCAG members purchased each week vegetables and fruit, tinned goods, dairy produce and household goods like soap and washing-up liquid at cost price from market gardeners and wholesalers. They were then sold at cost (some items were marked up with a small

addition to cover breakage and spillage) from a stall set up at the weekly social. Membership of the shopping club stood at over 60, and it assisted in a small, but direct, way to help fixed incomes to stretch further.

(Butcher *et al.*, 1980, pp. 27–8)

The working membership of SCAG numbers between ten and twelve (mostly pensioners). The group is predominantly female and working class and is organised on a formal basis with posts of chairperson, secretary, and so on.

Commentary on the group. One important aspect of this group is the support it received from the local Community Development Project. As well as receiving financial help in the form of grants, a worker from the project was heavily involved with SCAG for the first year of its existence, often convening and chairing meetings. Ten months after SCAG was formed officers were elected and the worker played no official role in the group. However, he continued to direct his energy into 'attempts to draw out the implications of ideas offered by members and to discourage early foreclosure of debate' (Butcher *et al.*, 1980, p. 34).

In terms of the group's success in combining pressure-group and self-help activities, the analysis by Butcher *et al.* is not optimistic. From this account it appears that SCAG leaned towards working on issues at a local level; indeed, 'wherever possible members opted to take self help and self organising initiatives rather than attempt to influence outside bodies or decision makers' (Butcher *et al.*, 1980, p. 41). The fact that many members viewed the source of their problems in factors external to the local community makes this preference for self-help of some interest. In their discussion of SCAG Butcher *et al.* suggest two reasons. First the group was able to secure grants from the community development project and was thus encouraged to search for solutions which could make use of this money. Second, although such money could in theory have been used to challenge external forces, opportunities for doing this were restricted. Local councillors were concerned with protecting their roles as advocates and spokespersons, and felt threatened by the rise of a group like SCAG.

For their part, group members were divided on how to challenge local councillors:

> The close-knit nature of community networks — in which councillors have often been personally known over long periods — also serves to inhibit action which is innovatory (in the sense of challenging norms governing people's relationships with their representatives). Divisions over strategy within SCAG sometimes reached stalemate because while on the one hand members would have liked to challenge the actions or opinions of particular councillors, on the other hand they felt inhibited from doing so because of personal ties and traditional normative expectations.

(Butcher et al., p. 41)

Local agencies were also adept at protecting their own interests and could do much to frustrate and delay proposals put forward by groups like SCAG. Even very modest ventures — if reliant on outside help — could take many months before successful implementation (the relatively straightforward small-jobs scheme, for example, took seven months from the time of the original discussions to completion of the first round of jobs). Such delays may favour the promotion of schemes which can be established quickly and which can be organised through the efforts of the pensioners themselves. The more protracted campaigns associated with pressure-groups activities may, in consequence, be abandoned.

Community work with the elderly: Small Heath[13]
In this example we turn to a more directive form of community work among older people. In 1978 the Victoria Residents' Association in Small Heath appointed a community worker to develop activities specifically with older people. The Small Heath district had undergone considerable change since its elderly residents had first moved in, with a noticeable deterioration both in housing conditions and community facilities in general. In some parts of the area plans for redevelopment have been in existence for a number of years, leaving residents in a state of uncertainty regarding the

future. In those areas where new estates had been built, pensioners – along with other residents – found a dearth of basic amenities (Victoria Residents' Association, 1979, p.4).

At the beginning of her appointment the community worker visited the existing pensioners' clubs in the Victoria area, building up contacts with elderly people she met there as well as visiting their neighbours. The residents' committee had no clear view of the range of activities she should attempt, hence the contacts she made with pensioners were vital in setting priorities for her work. From these discussions it became clear that a major problem was the limited provision for the housebound elderly. Two projects arose from this finding:

(1) A social club (both for the housebound as well as more active pensioners), held in a part of Small Heath where the transfer of pensioners to a new estate had led to problems of social isolation.

(2) A scheme was developed to encourage housebound or disabled pensioners to go out on their own. An arrangement was made for an account to be held with a local taxi firm. Each member of the scheme has a number of account slips, stamped by the residents' association, one of which is handed to the driver after each journey. The scheme is partly financed by members themselves and partly out of a subsidy providing transport for the disabled.

The community worker has also conducted advice sessions for pensioners, helped advise those who need to be rehoused, and prepared (with the local law centre) a handbook for older people in Small Heath. More recently she has planned (in conjunction with the Workers' Educational Association) a course on welfare rights for pensioners.

A further development has been the organisation of a pensioners' council in the Victoria district of Small Heath. This arose out of the community worker's need for more direct advice and support. The council meets monthly and has so far been involved in campaigns on issues affecting the elderly (the condition of pavements in the area), the organisation of social events, and the organisation of volunteers to help in emergencies affecting older people.

Commentary. This example from Small Heath illustrates the range of activities which community workers can develop with older people. The strength of this work lies in its capacity to secure improvements in the daily lives of individuals, particularly those whose who are isolated and who live on low incomes. One difficulty, however, in this form of community work concerns the bonds of dependency often formed between the group and the community worker involved. This arises from the division of labour between the 'professional' community worker and (in this instance) pensioners (a feature acknowledged by the worker in Small Heath). This dependency may limit the range of initiatives taken by older people, particularly as regards formal pressure-group activity.

The mounting of more direct political campaigns is also limited by the lack of ties between older people in Small Heath and organisations beyond the community. Activities with pensioners in other parts of Birmingham could, for example, increase the range of activities in which people were involved, as well as helping them to understand external influences on problems in the Small Heath area. The community worker is herself involved in a city-wide campaign for better pensions and welfare facilities, but she has found it difficult to involve on a regular basis pensioners in her area. The value of such regional links is explored in more detail in our last two case studies.

Political campaigns with the elderly: Tooting Action for Pensioners (TAP)[14]

In this third example we examine a branch of the BPTUAA. TAP was formed in the London borough of Tooting in 1973. The borough has a high proportion of older people (one in five), many of whom live in substandard housing. The group was organised after an initiative from a community worker employed by Task Force (a group formed in 1964 to develop voluntary and community work activities with pensioners). The worker visited a number of pensioners in the area, attempting to stimulate interest in the idea of an action group for pensioners. Despite only limited encouragement from these discussions, a public meeting attracting fifty pensioners was eventually held. Out of fifty, five people volunteered to set up a committee, four of these still being active members of TAP.

The aims of TAP are: (a) to act as voice for the pensioners in Tooting; (b) to work with others to effect improvements in facilities for pensioners in the area; (c) to build up community links and identity with the area as a whole; (d) to campaign for workshops and occupation for retired people; (e) to fight for improvements in the state retirement pension.

Since 1973 TAP has fought a number of campaigns. One of the most successful of these concerned the condition of pavements in the Tooting area. Using the abilities of a retired secretary and a retired photographer, examples of badly paved streets were documented; photographs were taken of the offending areas and comments were taken from pensioners who had experienced falls. This information was put together in booklet form by Task Force. Subsequently, TAP met representatives from the council and presented them with the booklet. Apart from a general improvement in pavements in the areas, TAP has won two cases of compensation for pensioners who have fallen in the streets.

Welfare rights work has been a central feature of TAP's activities. Working members have attended a course outlining the principles of supplementary benefits and they are involved in regular advice sessions for fellow-pensioners.

The group has also been active in campaigns on public expenditure cuts. A member of TAP was on picket duty throughout the struggle to prevent closure of a local geriatric hospital (St Benedict); he also collected over £200 in the Tooting area for members of the work-in committee. TAP has petitioned and lobbied councillors over the issue of spending cuts, as well as attending local and national demonstrations.

Commentary. One important feature of TAP concerns the organisational structure which has emerged. TAP has no standing committee, chairperson or secretary. During the week, working members handle individual cases and problems as they arise; unresolved problems and the planning of future campaigns are handled at weekly meetings of the group. Anyone may attend these meetings and become involved in its activities.

The success of TAP needs to be set within the context of the initial support provided by an outside community work agency. The importance of this support is illustrated if we look at the work of one of the earliest members of TAP — Ollie Hollingsworth. Together with a full-time job, she had been running a social club for elderly people in the area for twenty-one years. However, until the possibility of an action group was suggested by the Task Force worker, she had been content to work with older people purely on a social basis. She now feels, however, that involvement with TAP has expanded her life enormously, introducing her to a new range of skills: writing leaflets, representing claimants at social security tribunals, organising demonstrations, and so on.

Unfortunately, very few people seem to aspire to or achieve similar levels of involvement. From five working members in 1973, the group now has fifteen. Many more pensioners can be called upon to lobby local councillors or to attend regional or national demonstrations, but in terms of day-to-day organising the work-load falls on relatively few shoulders. At the present time (1982) the group is caught in a trap between, on the one hand, the ageing of its membership and the problem this creates for maintaining its level of activities, and on the other hand, the need to expand these activities in a context of public expenditure cuts and changes in social security legislation. In TAP's case, however, its integration within a national organisaton gives some reinforcement to its relatively small numbers. To conclude these case studies I shall now examine this larger organisation.

Political campaigns with the elderly: the Greater London Pensioners Trade Union Action Association (GLPTUAA)[15]

Tooting Action for Pensioners is a branch of the GLPTUAA, itself affiliated to the BPTUAA. The London region is one of the strongest groupings within the BPTUAA, a reflection of a militant tradition among pensioners in the London area. The organisation of local branches has most often been started by one or two pensioners along with community workers. They have usually attended luncheon clubs and day-centres, distributing leaflets and asking people to a meeting. After a discussion on problems affecting older people, the date of a subsequent meeting is announced; this may be attended by approximately fifteen people who will form the nucleus of a new branch. As well as running campaigns relevant to its own district, each branch will feed into national and regional campaigns. The GLPTUAA, for example, once organised a twenty-four-hour vigil outside Margaret Thatcher's house; it is also distributing a pensioners' charter with a list of minimum demands for restoring pensioners to a position of equality with other groups.

The significance of this work is that it is able to set the problems facing older people within a political framework. This can be illustrated by the following example from propaganda material produced by the GLPTUAA:

WHAT THATCHER HAS DONE. . .

For the Rich:
Enormous tax cuts for the already well-off and rich. Substantially increased the salaries of civil servants, MPs, armed forces, doctors and dentists.

For the Pensioners:
VAT and price increases while pensioners wait 6 months for their increases.
A refusal to link pensions with earnings which will mean further reductions in future pensions.
Savage cuts in public spending which mean Home Helps, Meals on Wheels, hospital care and holidays will all be slashed.

PENSIONERS CANNOT WAIT

Greater London Pensioners and Trades Union Action Committee demands that the pension be increased to half the average industrial male earnings for a single person, and three quarters for a couple. AS A FIRST STEP, we demand that the government uprate the pension IMMEDIATELY to half the average industrial male earnings for a couple, and a third for a single person (TUC policy).

This type of approach is particularly valuable given the way in which issues affecting pensioners have often been depoliticised. However, as we shall see below, the GLPTUAA face formidable organisational problems.

Commentary. The growth of the GLPTUAA, along with its national counterpart (the BPTUAA), illustrates a major change of emphasis within old-age politics. Existing pensioner organisations have been content to rely on traditional pressure-group methods, distancing themselves from picketing, street demonstrations, sit-ins, and other, more militant, tactics. However, although the GLPTUAA's turn towards greater militancy is to be weleomed, its diversification into new groups of pensioners will face major obstacles.

Organisations composed of elderly people may – because of illness and death – face a high turnover in their membership. Time and energy will need to be spent on recruiting new members and teaching them the ideas and methods the organisation is pursuing. This alone – when the core membership is small – may consume a disproportionate amount of time.

The time span needed for the achievement of political and economic goals must also be reckoned with. A man aged 70 can expect a further nine years of life, after 80 just five years. Where such goals seem remote, people's awareness about the possibility of their death (or serious illness) may cause them to feel that involvement in political life is futile.

Both of the above points are reinforced by aspects of the material world facing older people. Low income, poor housing and deteriorating public services may cause feelings of great bitterness. Such feelings may, it is true, generate an anger capable of finding political expression. But people may also react with a sense of betrayal, feeling rejected by a labour movement whose activities and goals no longer reflect their own experiences of life. In this respect, the elderly represent a group both within and outside the working class: a huge group of trade unionists who no longer have a trade union. People may not lose their identities as workers, but the insecurities accompanying old age may lead to significant changes in consciousness. Although still supportive of the labour movement at one level, many older people may become hostile to groups who are allegedly damaging their material interests. The problem here is one of access to alternative explanations. Older people spend significantly less of their time out of doors (in pubs, clubs, etc.) than other age groups, and hence become reliant on the media for interpretations of political disputes. This reliance may, in turn, reinforce their isolation and lack of involvement.

Support from trade unionists and community workers may do much to ease the obstacles described and in the work of the Gray Panthers and some of the British groups described in this chapter one can find a clear indication of the potential for radicalisation among the elderly. But, accepting that this might be possible, what is the most likely form a politics of ageing will take? What will be the social composition of old-age movements?

CONCLUDING COMMENTS

In this chapter I have tried to argue that various forms of political action may take place among older people. I have argued that increased age does not place insuperable obstacles to involvement in political activity. Constraints are undoubtedly present for many sections of the elderly population, but these should demand new ideas and strategies rather than blanket dismissal.

Does this mean, however, that older people will emerge as a homogeneous political force, demanding – in one voice – clearly defined economic and social changes? Historically, old age movements have rarely been broad coalitions of economic classes. The Towsend movement, for example, was 'heavily middle class' (Fischer, 1977); the more radical British organisations, on the other hand, have been predominantly working class. In terms of understanding these divisions, two points are of crucial importance:

(1) It is a mistake to see either retirement or old age removing life-long differences in income and social status. Arguably, since the early postwar period, pensioners have been affected by new forms of stratification: particularly in respect of occupational pensions. As we argued in Chapter 2, these differences are likely to increase over the next two decades, as the 1975 social security legislation introduces divisions between those who are and those who are not elegible for the new pension. Moreover, this legislation has transferred income inequalities directly into the pension system (via earnings-related benefits). As Jeffreys has argued:

> It is bad enough to live in a society where people can command higher salaries because of the marketability of their particular skill, and because of advantages in their sex, race, and background. It will be pernicious to live in a society where the Government, as well as private pension schemes, will allow people increased money in retirement because of these factors.
>
> (*New Society*, 28 August , 1975)

(2) These economic divisions in old age are likely to be reinforced by social factors. One of the most important of these is the limited group identification among older people. Given the unattractive stereotypes attached to old age, older people may resist identification with senior citizens' groups, etc. This may be particularly characteristic of the middle-class elderly, whose income and/or ownership or property is more likely to lift them above the poverty line.

Do these material and social factors lead one to reject the likelihood of a significant pensioners' organisation developing? This position is, I think, too pessimistic. Under the terms of the 1975 social security legislation, no radical change in the living standards of pensioners is likely to occur before the beginning of the next century. Moreover, the position of older people may be further undermined, given the possibility of a worsening of the early 1980s' recession and attempts to reduce still further health and welfare services. Both of these factors are likely to strengthen militant tendencies among pensioner organisations, and to question the adequacy of traditional pressure-group tactics. In addition, the growth in the number of retired people (via demographic and labour-market pressures) is likely to lead to a broadening in the range of issues encompassed by pensioner groups (e.g. the treatment of old age in the mass media, the access of elderly people to cultural and educational resources). As in the case of the women's movement, pensioners will demand both changes in their material status and in their position as a subordinate social group. The argument for freedom from stereotypes of ageing may become as politically and morally compelling as existing slogans in the struggle for women's liberation (indeed, given that the bulk of activists in pensioner groups are women, the two movements share much common ground).

To summarise the argument so far. The type of pensioner organisations most likely to emerge will be built along class lines or around single-issue campaigns. Broad coalitions may, for example, be built around campaigns over the adequacy of health and education facilities in retirement; conversely, campaigns to improve the state retirement pension may only attract working-class support. Whatever the social base, however, political action by and on behalf of elderly people is likely to become increasingly common.

9

Capitalism, Socialism and the Construction of Old Age

In this concluding chapter an interpretation will be presented of social influences on the characteristics of old age and retirement. These have been discussed under various headings throughout the book. I have examined the connections between the emergence of retirement and the political economy of capitalism; considered difficulties in the transition from work to retirement, for both men and women; documented the struggle over questions of income security and social welfare; and, finally, reviewed the politics of ageing and the role of organised groups of pensioners.

Underlying the presentation of these themes has been a concern to relate the dominant features associated with growing old to the political economy of Western capitalism. In this respect the approach has been similar to that followed by Guillemard:

> Our approach, then, is an attempt to meet the question of the social production of old age. It is less concerned with studying the characteristics of old age than with examining the production of these characteristics by the social system.
> (Guillemard, 1981, pp. 2–3)

In this final chapter I shall summarise key features of the relationship between old age and capitalism, focusing upon: (a) capitalism in crisis; (b) the historical development of capitalism; and (c) the relationship between productive and non-productive personnel. Finally, I shall examine the question of socialism and old age, concluding with a series of questions on the nature of a socialist social policy for the elderly.

CAPITALISM IN CRISIS

If one analyses the various studies concerned with the history of old age, a distinctive feature to emerge is the importance of material factors in determining the social position of older people. Thomas, in *Age and Authority in Early Modern England*, finds a 'hostility towards those who opted out of the economic process and reluctance to devote much of society's resources to their maintenance' (1976, p. 237). He goes on: 'outside their own families the relief of the elderly poor was a low priority and in the village it could be bitterly resented' (1976, p. 242).

In conditions such as these, one historian (Macfarlane, 1970) sees an explanation for the phenomenon of witchcraft. Groups such as elderly women were particularly vulnerable to accusations of witchcraft, and the incidence of such accusations may well have increased during periods of economic distress. Macfarlane, in his study *Witchcraft in Tudor and Stuart England*, sketches the background to this in the following way:

> population growth and changes in ownership created a group of poorer villagers whose ties to their slightly wealthier neighbours became more tenuous. People increasingly had to decide whether to invest their wealth in maintaining the old at a decent standard of living or in improvements which would keep them abreast of their yeoman neighbours ... During the period between 1560 and 1650 the internal institutions which had dealt with the old and poor, church relief, the manorial organisation and neighbourly and kinship ties were strained. People still felt enforced to help and support each other, while also feeling the necessity to invest their capital in buying land and providing for their children. The very poor were not the problem. They could be whipped and sent on their way, or hired as labourers. It was the slightly less affluent

neighbours or kin who only demanded a little help who
became an increasing source of anxiety. To refuse them
was to break a web of long-held values.

(Macfarlane, 1970, pp. 205–6)

Macfarlane suggests that the phenomenon of witchcraft may
have been a response to a growth in the number of elderly
dependants at a time of economic difficulty. In place of out-
right refusal of help withcraft prosecution may have allowed
communities to sever 'long-held' obligations and commit-
ments.

The impact on the elderly of disturbances in the economy
have hardly been lessened with the emergence of a mature
capitalist economy. In the depression of the 1930s we find
elderly people caught between the contradiction of inadequate
pensions but intense social pressure to retire and make way
for the young. Within families, the crisis of mass unemployment caused much soul-searching — and this has been scarcely
documented by social historians — about how support could
be maintained to both older and younger generations.

Moving ahead to our own time, large-scale unemployment
is again raising issues about the obligations of society and the
state towards the elderly, their right to employment and to
inflation-proofed incomes being important subjects for
debate.

These examples serve to illustrate the point that the lives
of older people are inseparable from a web of economic
relationships and it is these relationships which must be
considered primary in influencing both the way in which we
think about the process of growing old and the position of
older people within the social structure.

In the twentieth century, periods of crises of over-produc-
tion, labour shortages or surpluses, or the chaos of war, have
created a range of images through which old age is viewed.
The appearance is one of a progression from abject poverty
to retirement as a new style of life, with leisure activities and
creative hobbies. The reality, however, has been one of quite
violent shifts in the social acceptability of permanently with-
drawing from the labour force. In the 1950s, in Britain at
least, retirement was interpreted in pathogenic terms, as a

period which would bring misery for the individual and prove a burden for the economy. In the early 1980s, by contrast, it appears, along with temporary youth employment schemes, to be the state's only solution (as it was the Labour Party's in the 1930s) to mass unemployment. The subordination of retirement to the economy must, however, be seen within the context of the overall development of capitalism.

RETIREMENT AND THE DEVELOPMENT OF CAPITALISM

The emergence of retirement as a social institution has been heavily influenced by capitalist social relations. Graebner, in a major study of the history of retirement in the USA, has traced its development to

> the changing methodologies of American capitalism in the nineteenth and twentiety centuries. Voluntary retirement . . . was appropriate to small-scale, pre-corporate business units typical of entrepreneurial capitalism . . . [with the rise of the corporation] organized systems of mandatory retirement now seemed possible (because the working class was organized into a more manageable unit) as well as more necessary. For leaders in business, labor, and the professions, retirement became a panacea for the ills that beset their particular fields. For business, retirement meant reduced unemployment, lower rates of turnover, a younger, more efficient, and more conservative workforce; for labor, it was in part a way of transferring work from one generation to another in industries with a surplus of workers.
>
> (Graebner, 1980, p. 13)

In this analysis, the emergence of retirement becomes part of the 'reconstitution of the labour force', with the 'removal . . . of those segments least capable of adapting to the work requirements of a labour process designed for capital accumulation' (Miles, 1981, p. 8). With this approach, therefore, the old are sacrificed in the corporation's drive for order and efficiency: speed-ups on the line, work-measurement techniques, etc., sealing the fate of the ageing worker.

As the work of Thane (1978) has demonstrated, the quest for efficiency and productivity has also been important in the British history of pensions and retirement. However, it may also be the case that American capitalism (via the rise of large-scale industrial organisation) carried out an earlier debate on the effectiveness of the older worker. Indicative of this is the development of retirement preparation schemes (from the late 1940s onwards), a phenomenon which, in the case of Britain, developed both later (from the mid-1950s) and at a much slower rate. National differences are further illustrated by the contrasting attitudes displayed towards retirement by American and British workers. American surveys from the 1950s onwards suggest more positive feelings towards retirement. In Britain, on the other hand, only since the late 1960s have studies begun to report a more significant shift from the highly negative views reported by research in the 1950s. A number of political and economic reasons can be advanced for these differences: the absence of labour shortages in the USA in the 1950s; the early development of assembly-line methods of work (Orbach has analysed the tendency in the 1950s for automobile workers to retire before the compulsory age of retirement);[1] differences in pension and social security arrangements.

Crucial to both countries, however, is the economic relation as a controlling factor in the emergence of retirement as a social institution. These relations have set definite limits to the growth of retirement, limits which can be expressed more precisely in terms of the tensions between productive and non-productive sectors in the economy.

RETIREMENT: THE ATTITUDES OF THE STATE AND THE COMMUNITY

In understanding the form taken by state policies towards the elderly, it is useful to reflect upon the overall significance of older people for capitalism. We have already suggested (see Chapter 6) that compared with the role of the current and future work-force the elderly are less essential to the needs of capital. Concern about their limited potential for the economy has been an important strand in postwar social policy. Writing in the late 1940s Hubback argued:

> From the point of view of the community it is indeed far more encouraging to spend money on children, since this expenditure can be regarded as a hopeful investment, than to spend it on old people — desirable as this may be from the point of view of individual happiness.
>
> (Hubback, 1947, p. 134)

The Royal Commission on Population saw the problem in the following way:

> the burden of maintaining the old does not consist in the money paid out as Old Age Pensions. It consists in the excess of the consumption by the old over their production. It is the fact that (with some exceptions) the old consume without producing which differentiates them from the active population and makes of them a factor reducing the average standard of living of the community.
>
> (Royal Commission on Population, 1949, p. 113)

It is difficult to read these and more recent reports written about the elderly without concluding that concern about their 'lack of productivity' is still highly influential in shaping state policies. In a speech to accountants and managers of pension funds, the Chancellor of the Exchequer Sir Geoffrey Howe questioned the readiness of today's workers to provide for the retired, sick and disabled. According to *The Guardian* report:

> In somewhat inelegant language — 'nothing is for nothing' — the Chancellor suggested that working people may have reached the point beyond which they would not be prepared to increase their contributions to the pensions of the retired. There was, he suggested, a new 'affordability' factor to be weighed in the pension debate.
>
> Three developments were identified by the Chancellor as the cause of this possible taxpayers' revolt: the increase in pensions (a 30 per cent rise in real value between 1971

and 1981), the increase in the number of pensioners (from 13.5 per cent of the population in 1951 to 17.5 per cent today) and our low economic growth.

(*The Guardian*, 10 June 1981)

This 'affordability' factor is certainly not new. Thus in both feudal and capitalist societies one can find evidence of communities questioning their obligations to groups such as the elderly. Under capitalism, however, two significant developments have taken place. First, as we saw in Chapter 2, improvements in life expectancy have contributed to an ageing of the population. Second, retirement has developed as a social institution functional to the needs of capitalism, with only those willing to act as cheap labour or possessing a required skill being able to remain in work. There are contradictory features about the way in which society and the state views this withdrawal from the labour market.

On the one hand, there are positive features which both can identify. Younger workers may see retirement as a legitimate means of increasing their own opportunities for work (Carliner, 1969); and this view may be internalised by older workers themselves. Retirement may be viewed both by the family and the community as providing possibilities for voluntary work. By remaining useful for as long as possible, older people may help to earn guarantees for support in their own period of dependency. For capitalism, the institution of retirement may serve a number of functions:

In the advanced capitalist societies, the social production of marginality and dependency in the later phases of the life cycle may serve a function in terms of . . . removing excess manpower from the competition for jobs, and as a foundation for the generation of large investment pools providing capital funds for both the private sector and the state . . . Moreover, by fostering dependency on the state, people are induced to grant legitimacy and stability to the state as guarantor of their future security.

(Marshall, 1981, pp. 98–9)

On the other hand, we can also identify a number of tensions in the relationship of the retired and elderly to both the state and the community.

For the family, the crisis in the welfare state, combined with the increase in the numbers of the very elderly, will result in pressure to meet responsibilities towards older people. The financial implications of this, however, may be increasingly difficult to accept in a context of large-scale unemployment. At such times, forms of control and discrimination against the elderly may be applied with increasing rigour. For those older people who become dependent on their families for support, a considerable sacrifice may be made in terms of their individuality. Harassed daughters may treat the elderly as children, since both are identified as increasing the domestic work-load. It may also be the case that daughters find the role of caring for their mothers a threatening and disturbing experience: first, because of the connotations for their own future dependency; and second, because it subverts the mother's identity as a care-giver (Evers, 1981, makes a similar point in relation to women caring for female geriatric patients).

At the level of the state, we find a contradiction in the experience of retirement at an economic level, and the planning for retirement in terms of social and cultural resources. The limited development of these resources has done most harm to the working-class elderly. For them, the absence of savings and a reasonable occupational pension means dependency both upon state provision and on state definitions of what constitutes an acceptable old age. For the middle class, on the other and, its control over property and significant amounts of savings and good occupational pensions, all mean that the middle-class elderly usually live well above the state minimum. Even in extreme old age, middle-class old people are likely to end their days in superior homes (and to keep out of hospitals more often), thus escaping the worst effects of discrimination by the state against the elderly. From birth until death, in fact, the influence of class continues to exert a disproportionate effect, both on the quality of life and on the quantity of resources which people receive.

SOCIALIST CONSTRUCTION AND OLD AGE

Finally, I want briefly to examine the position of the elderly in non-capitalist societies, taking examples from two 'socialist' countries. There are grounds, I would argue, for believing that socialism can bring significant improvements to the lives of older people. The building of a socialist democracy, the grad-ual dissolution of the division between physical and intellec-tual labour, the abandonment of the profit motive: all these changes are likely to bring major benefits to the position of the elderly. As Broyelle comments: 'when a society is no longer driven by profit, when it no longer measures produc-tivity as a function of profitability, its relation to its formerly "unproductive" members is radically altered. It doesn't give charity because its need for them is as great as their need for it' (1977, pp. 128–9).

Beyond these general comments, however, lie issues of enormous complexity. Marxists have, in general, failed to identify the broad outlines of a socialist social policy.[2] Still less have they considered the position of specific groups such as the elderly and disabled within the context of socialism. However, given that most European countries have between 15–20 per cent of their populations over the age of 60, the role of the elderly in the transition to socialism may become critical. Two features merit particular attention.

First, all socialist revolutions have faced pressure in areas such as housing, medicine and food supplies. In a context of social and economic upheaval, there is a strong possibility of older people being pushed aside in the face of urgent tasks of defence and survival, the likelihood being increased where there is no economic and social policy for the elderly.

Second, even if there are no major problems in the organi-sation of health and social services there will be important tasks in connection with reorganising the economy along socialist lines. Questions such as democracy within the work-place, the roles of men and women at home and at work, are likely to come to the centre of discussion. By contrast, there may be only limited consideration given to the needs of those who no longer play a central role in the economy.

Before outlining the type of questions a socialist welfare

policy will need to consider, I shall first review the experience of present-day 'socialist' societies.

SOCIALIST SOCIETIES AND OLD AGE

I shall examine the largest 'socialist' countries — the Soviet Union and China — *vis-à-vis* my analysis of policies towards the elderly. Two problems must be faced in producing even a brief review. First, the characterisation of these societies is itself a subject of widespread debate. Corrigan *et al.*, for example, describe the Soviet Union and China as '*contradictory* social formations, in which socialism is dominant but not triumphant, and capitalism is subordinate, but not vanquished' (1978, p. 147). Given such an analysis, one would also expect contradictory features in the area of social policy. In the case of the Soviet Union, for example, one can point to guarantees of work and the existence of a statutory minimum wage and pensions. On the other hand, there is little evidence that relationships between users and providers have been transformed in the direction of greater participation and democracy in the planning of health and social services. Moreover, in the area of housing and social security, the nuclear family remains the principal unit of organisation — a feature which discriminates against groups such as the elderly (Deacon, 1981).

A second problem facing any review of the elderly under 'socialism' lies in the paucity of research. Mention of the elderly can be found in a number of general texts on the Soviet Union and China, and a limited amount of research has been completed. However, while it may be possible to make quantitative judgements about the position of older people (range of statutory services, retirement policies, etc.), qualitative statements about their relationship to society as a whole will be more difficult to substantiate.

At a very general level, discussions about material conditions in these societies invariably mentions the dramatic improvements in life expectancy (a consequence of major falls in infant mortality). Moreover, general campaigns to improve health have undoubtedly had an important effect on the care of the elderly. However, at least in the case of the Soviet Union, there is some evidence to suggest that health care for older people comes fairly low in medical priorities (geriatrics is not recognised as a speciality in its own right), and that greater attention is given to those making a 'contribution towards national efficiency and economic growth' (Ryan, 1978, p. 132).

In both countries there has been the development of specific 'privileges' for older people. In the Soviet Union Chebotarev and Sachuk (1980) identify low-rent housing and help with repairs, inexpensive public transportation and easy access to cultural and leisure facilities. In the case of China both Broyelle (1977) and Treas (1979) argue that attempts have been made to increase the social and political involvement of older people. According to Treas:

> retirees participate in the programs of political study. Indeed, their involvement is highly valued, because they serve to remind the younger generations of the difficult life before the Socialist Revolution. Retirees may also investigate citizen complaints – serving in para-police and judicial capacities while arbitrating marital disputes and differences between neighbors. In fact, the aged are prominent members of the Street Committees which organize far reaching programs of social control, social service, and political indoctrination. Even at the prestigious May 7th Cadre School (where leaders of the Eastern Municipal District of Peking are trained), students include some men and women in their 60s.
>
> (Treas, 1979, p. 41)

These general observations are not based on detailed and long-term investigations, hence it is difficult to gauge their reliability. It is even more difficult to speculate on the quality of relationships experienced by the elderly. In the case of China a number of observers (e.g. Worsley, 1975; Kinoy, 1979) have commented on the continued strength of family ties. A rise in female employment has also opened a role for older people in caring for their grandchildren and in performing general household tasks for sons and daughters. However, a possible strain in the performance of these roles has been indicated by Davin (1976). Analysing changes in family relationships during the 1950s, she writes:

> While her son's wife was out at work, the older woman would look after the grandchildren and do menial tasks which would once have been the special duties of the younger woman. She cooked for the family, including her daughter-in-law, who would formerly have had to serve her. The symbolism of this reversal of roles was certainly not lost on a people who lived in a society loaded with symbolism. The older women were, not surprisingly, often resentful. In the 1950s publications for women carried much that was clearly directed at this unlucky generation of middle-aged women, reminding them that in enabling their daughters-in-law to work, they were themselves making a contribution to the welfare of society and to that of the family.
>
> (Davin, 1976, pp. 125–6)

There is a tension here between the gains for younger women in being able to enter occupational roles, and the allocation to older women of a new range of domestic tasks. Although these can provide a social anchor to the experience of growing old, they may come to be experienced as a constraint where alternative roles are unavailable. Another important question concerns policies towards retirement. This issue needs to be placed in the context of the overwhelming importance of rural life in both countries. Thus it has been argued that in the case of agriculture it is possible (and in many cases expected) for older workers to remain an important part of the production unit. Some writers, in fact, give an idyllic picture of workers gradually reducing their productive capacities in line with changes in their physical stamina.[3] Once again, however, in the absence of reliable surveys, it is difficult to arrive at firm conclusions.

In the case of retirement policies in the industrial sector, the picture is rather complex. The role of pensioners in relieving labour shortages has certainly been debated in the Eastern bloc countries. In the Soviet Union, for example, inducements to the elderly to remain at work have taken a number of forms. Smirnov has described changes to the pension system in the 1960s whereby

> Most employed pensioners . . . became entitled to half their full pension, while in the Urals, Siberia and the Far East, where the demand for labour was most acute, they were entitled to as much as 75 per cent, with a ceiling of 200 roubles a month for pension and wage combined. In agriculture, where older workers can make a particularly useful contribution, full pensions became payable, so that, in one way or another, the pension actually paid began to depend on all sorts of factors – where the pensioner lived, his wage, his trade or occupation, and the particular branch of activity in which he worked or in which his job was classified.
>
> (Smirnov, 1977, p. 92)

The absence of significant unemployment in the Soviet Union undoubtedly removes one source of pressure upon the elderly. It would, however, be interesting to know something of the treatment of older workers in conditions of localised unemployment.

In the case of China, Treas makes a number of important points in relation to manpower policies and older workers. Provision for lighter work may be available for those workers who are below retirement age and in a poor state of health. However, she also observed that

> those lower paid workers with fewer skills are 'encouraged' to retire as early as age 50. It may well be that they are leaving none-too-rewarding jobs for comfortable pensions and more enjoyable leisure, family life, and community participation. None the less, retirement policies in the industrial sector suggest that high status is more closely associated with skills and education than with age.
>
> (Treas, 1979, p. 42)

These examples serve to illustrate the type of problems which may face older people in the period of socialist construction. Now I want to consider the components of a socialist welfare policy for the elderly.

A SOCIALIST SOCIAL POLICY FOR THE ELDERLY: SOME KEY QUESTIONS

There are a number of major questions and issues around which a socialist policy for the elderly could be developed. These can be identified as follows:

(1) What are the economic mechanisms available for ensuring an equal allocation of resources both to workers and non-workers? How can the ideology of the pensioner as a *dependant* be replaced in favour of a social status emphasising his or her equality with all other social groups?

(2) What is the place of retirement in a socialist society? It is argued by some that it will become less common, as workers move from job to job, in line with changes in their physical stamina and mental aptitude. However, we need to identify the social and occupational factors which could assist this transformation. What impact would this have in the organisation of work? What would be the implications for wider economic objectives?

(3) What is the political role of older people in a socialist society? This is an issue of great importance to social policy, because the way it is answered will do much to clarify the range of social roles available to older people. Is their political role simply to be that of memories of the past, educating the younger generation about previous injustices and struggles? Alternatively, can we identify more specific tasks for older people in the construction of socialism, tasks which refer not only to the past but also to the present and the future?[4]

(4) How would elderly people relate to cultural and educational institutions? Would these continue to be monopolised by the young or those from white-collar occupations? Alternatively, will the elderly, and particularly those engaged in manual work, come to participate both in equal numbers and on equal terms?

(5) What are the new types of social relations which, following Deacon (1981) and Wilson (1981), a socialist social policy needs to develop? Deacon has identified the following changes:

> The relationships between users and providers, producers and consumers, helpers and helped, administrators and receivers, would be transformed beyond recognition. The relationships would not be bureaucratic, not that of professional to client, not sexist or racist. Additionally it can be concluded that social policy would dominate economic policy and social policy would become a matter of realisation of human potential, the possibility of this potential being realisable because men and women would no longer be dominated by commodity fetishism.
>
> (Deacon, 1981, p. 52)

This approach has enormous implications for older people. The bureaucratic organisation of many old people's homes and geriatric hospitals indicates how the *quality* as well as the *quantity* of services is an important issue for discussion. Older people do need improved health services, better pensions, different types of housing and a variety of aids when they become disabled. But they also need a *reason* for using these things. In our society the purpose of life in old age is often unclear. The way this period is described in social policy often underlines the experience. Old age is seen as a 'problem', with the elderly viewed as dependants; worse still, they are often described as a non-productive burden upon the economy. Such categories have generated their own language of impotence and despair. The aim of a socialist social policy must be to make a decisive break from this environment. We need policies which will make growing old a natural part of the life-cycle, rather than one which is experienced as wholly unnatural and to be feared.

SUMMARY

We can summarise the main arguments developed in this book in the following way: the experience of growing old must be viewed as an event heavily influenced by class and gender relations; to view it as a period where the biological process of age assumes a primary role is to ignore the cumulative power and significance of life in a class society; similarly, the form which experiences in retirement take (tensions in the transition from work to retirement; poverty in old age) are not a consequence of individual characteristics or the process of ageing, but reflect the influence of numerous forms of inequality within capitalism; ideologies of retirement and the care of the elderly within homes and hospitals thus become examples of the way in which growing old is constructed through a range of policies imposed upon the older population.

We have only just begun to appreciate the full extent to which a society divided along the lines of class and gender influences life-chances and experiences from birth to death. The extent of inequality in areas such as the family, education and work were among the first to be analysed by sociologists and others. To these areas we may add a fourth: retirement and old age. In many ways, inequality and oppression in old age symbolises the fundamental weaknesses of social policy and social welfare in a capitalist society.

Endnotes

CHAPTER 2

1. These figures are for the United Kingdom (see *Social Trends*, no. 11, 1981).
2. See Walker (1980) for a comprehensive review of studies on poverty and dependency in old age.
3. These data are taken from Bosanquet (1978).
4. Owen (1977) has provided a succinct review of health issues confronting the elderly.

CHAPTER 3

1. This chapter is a revised version of an earlier paper (Phillipson, 1977).
2. Ensor saw the elderly in the following way:

> for the mainstay purposes of the nation, whether production in peace-time or defence in war-time, I am afraid that nearly all of them must be rated as passengers, not crew. Therefore their enormous increase . . . so far from mitigating the loss of those three million young adults, actually makes it worse, since there is a much larger burden for the few shoulders to carry.
>
> (Ensor, 1950, p. 129)

3. These surveys are discussed in the review by Stevenson (1977).
4. Rowntree said of the old-age pensioners living below the poverty line that 'They are, indeed, the poorest people in the city. Of course, they *do* get an occasional ounce of tobacco, or a glass of beer, but only by suffering a little more from cold or undernourishment. A poor, drab ending to a life' (quoted in Stevenson, 1977, p. 81).

CHAPTER 4

1. Evidence on this point is provided by Lunn and Waters (1969). Since their study the age at which miners can retire has been lowered to 60. Their findings remain, however, of considerable interest.
2. In a study of the long-term unemployed, Adrian Sinfield notes: 'Workers approaching retirement age experience the highest long-term unemployment. Generally, both the rate of long-term unemployment and the proportion of unemployed who are long out of work rises with increasing age' (Sinfield, 1968, p. 30; see also Showler and Sinfield, 1981).
3. Unless stated otherwise all quotations are taken from Phillipson (1978).
4. For a useful discussion on this theme see Dumazedier (1974).

CHAPTER 5

1. See, for example, Burgess (1960) and Stearns (1977).
2. For some exceptions, see Heyman and Jeffers (1968), Lipman (1961) and Kerckhoff (1966).
3. For British research on the menopause see Fairhurst (1979); for a major American study on widowhood see Lopata (1979).
4. See Gardiner (1981) for a more detailed analysis on how women have been affected by the recession.
5. For a collection of studies on the theme of housework see Malos (1980).
6. See, in particular, Jacobsohn (1970), Streib and Schneider (1971), and Fox (1977).
7. See Crawford (1971) for evidence of this.

CHAPTER 6

1. This chapter draws on the work of Means (1980), Brown (1972), Parker (1965) and Townsend and Wedderburn (1965).
2. For a review of issues on the elderly in homes and in sheltered housing see Plank (1978).
3. For a review of the development of sheltered housing see Butler *et al.*, (1979). For a discussion on 'very sheltered housing' see Harbridge (1980).
4. See the exchange between the Prime Minister and Dame Irene Ward, *Hansard*, vol. 652, cols 892–3, 1962.

5. The entire debate on National Insurance and National Assistance Benefits is highly revealing regarding government attitudes towards the elderly. See *Hansard*, vol. 655, cols 1142–50, 1962.

6. For additional information see copies of *Fightback*; see also the Association of Directors of Social Services (1980). For information on cuts in the NHS see *Labour Research* (February 1980); also, the *Politics of Health Group*, No. 2 (no date). The effect of cuts in the home-help service has been reviewed by Harbridge in *Community Care* (13 December 1979). COHSE's 1981 paper *In Defence of the Old* reports on a number of campaigns against the closure of geriatric hospitals.

7. The Personal Social Services Council has itself become a victim of the public expenditure cuts.

CHAPTER 7

1. For a comprehensive review of the elderly and the use of social services, see Age Concern (1981).

2. See, for example, Taylor *et al.* (1973) and Willis (1977).

3. For a detailed review and bibliography on this area see Knox (1980).

CHAPTER 8

1. Some of the ideas explored in this chapter were developed in an earlier article (Phillipson, 1980).

2. This debate is arising out of the demand to equalise pension ages; however, the present recession is being used to strengthen the case for raising women's retirement age, instead of lowering that for men.

3. The following account draws extensively on the work of Fischer (1977); see also Putman (1970).

4. See Pratt (1974) for a review of the development of these organisations.

5. The following summary is taken from Gray Panthers (1976).

6. For a brief history of the Federation see Dunn (no date).

7. See Castle (1980, p. 102).

8. See Buckingham *et al.* (1979) for a summary of these developments.

9. Like the NFOAPA, the BPTUAA also publishes its own paper — *The British Pensioner*.

10. The Transport & General Workers' Union has its own pensioners' organisation with a full-time secretary and researcher.

11. For one of the few discussions on community work and the elderly see Buckingham *et al.* (1979). For additional information see Jones *et al.* (forthcoming) and Erskine and Phillipson (1980).
12. The Cleator Moor example draws on the work of Butcher *et al.* (1980).
13. Most of the material reported in this case study is from an interview with Ann Hindley, the community worker with the project.
14. The material in this section draws on an interview with Ollie Hollingsworth, a found member of TAP.
15. The material in this section draws on an interview with Cecil Sharpley, Chairperson of the GLPTUAA.

CHAPTER 9

1. Cited in Friedmann and Orbach (1974).
2. See Deacon (1981), however, for a recent discussion on this theme.
3. See, for example, Broyelle (1977, p. 125).
4. Of course, there is a certain irony in a plea of this kind. Both China and the Soviet Union appear dominated by elderly people at the top echelons of power. In this instance, age is clearly not a factor disqualifying people from major political responsibilities. My argument is directed at the mass of elderly people who — by virtue of institutionalised retirement and the operation of pension schemes — may be denied full access to social and political rights. We are not arguing in favour of a gerontocracy or even discrimination in favour of the elderly. The view being put forward is that older people should have equal rights with other major groups in society to participate in political, cultural and social institutions.

References

Abel-Smith, B. (1964) *The Hospitals* (London: Heinemann).

Abel-Smith, B. and Townsend, P. (1962) *The Poor and the Poorest* (London: Bell & Sons).

Abrams, M. (1978) *Beyond Three Score and Ten: A First Report of a Survey of the Elderly* (London: Age Concern).

Abrams, M. (1979) 'The Future of the Elderly', *Futures*, June 1979, pp. 178–84.

Abrams, M. (1980) *Beyond Three Score and Ten: A Second Report of a Survey of the Elderly* (London: Age Concern).

Abrams, M. (1978) 'Time and the Elderly', *New Society*, 21–28 December 1978, pp. 685–6.

Abrams, M. & O'Brien, J. (1981) *Political Attitudes and Ageing in Britain* (London: Age Concern).

Age Concern (1974) *The Attitudes of the Retired and Elderly* (London: Age Concern).

Age Concern (1977–81) *Profiles of the Elderly*, vols 1–3, 1977; vol. 4, 1978; vol. 5, 1980; vol. 6, 1981 (London: Age Concern).

Alderman, G. (1978) *British Elections: Myth and Reality* (London: Batsford).

Anderson, M. (1971) *Family Structure in Nineteenth Century Lancashire* (Cambridge University Press).

Anderson, W. F. and Cowan, N. (1956) 'Work and Retirement: Influences on the Health of Older Men', *The Lancet*, 29 December 1956, pp. 1344–7.

Association of Directors of Social Services (1980) *Cuts in Public Expenditure* (Newcastle: ADSS).

Batchelor, L. R. C. and Napier, M. B. (1953) 'Attempted Suicide in Old Age', *British Medical Journal*, 28 November 1953, pp. 1186–90.

Baum, M. and Baum, R. C. (1980) *Growing Old: A Societal Perspective* (Englewood Cliffs, N. J.: Prentice-Hall).

Beauvoir, S. de (1966) *A Very Easy Death* (London: Deutsch and Weidenfeld & Nicolson).

Beauvoir, S. de (1972) *Old Age* (London: Deutsch and Weidenfeld & Nicolson).

Bebbington, A. C. (1979) 'Changes in the Provision of Social Services to the Elderly in the Community over Fourteen Years', *Social Policy and Administration*, vol. 13, no. 2, pp. 111–23.

Bengston, V. L. *et al.* (1969) 'Occupational Differences in Retirement: Patterns of Role-activity and Life-outlook among Chicago Teachers and Steel-workers', in Havighurst *et al.*, (1969).

Beveridge Report (1942) *Social Insurance and Allied Services* (London: HMSO).

Beynon, H. and Wainwright, H. (1979) *The Workers' Report on Vickers* (London: Pluto Press).

Binstock, R. H. (1974) 'Ageing and the Future of American Politics', *Annals of the American Academy of Political Sciences*, vol. 415, pp. 201–12.

Blackburn, R. (1976) 'Marxism: Theory of Proletarian Revolution', *New Left Review*, no. 97, pp. 3–35.

Blondel, J. (1966) *Voters, Parties and Leaders* (Harmondsworth: Penguin).

Blythe, R. (1979) *The View in Winter: Reflections on Old Age* (London: Allen Lane).

Bosanquet, N. (1978) *A Future for Old Age* (London: Temple Smith/New Society).

Bottomore, T. B. and Rubel, M. (1974) *Karl Marx: Selected Writings in Sociology and Social Philosophy* (Harmondsworth: Penguin).

Boucher, C. A. (1957) *Survey of Services Available to the Chronic Sick and the Elderly*, Ministry of Health, Reports on Public Health and Medical Subjects No. 98 (London: HMSO).

Branson, N. and Heinemann, M. (1971) *Britain in the Nineteen Thirties* (London: Weidenfeld & Nicolson).

Braverman, H. (1974) *Labor and Monopoly Capitalism* (New York: Monthly Review Press).

Brearley, P. (1975) *Social Work, Ageing and Society* (London: Routledge & Kegan Paul).

Breckenridge, E. L. (1953) *Effective use of Older Workers* (Chicago: Wilcox & Follett; reprinted New York: Arno Press, 1980).

Brocklehurst, J. C. (ed.) (1978) *Textbook of Geriatric Medicine*, 2nd edn (Edinburgh: Churchill).

Brown, M. (1972) 'The Development of Local Authority Welfare Services from 1948–1965 under Part III of the National Assistance Act', University of Manchester Ph.D. thesis.

Broyelle, C. (1977) *Women's Liberation in China* (Brighton: Harvester Press).

Buckingham, G. *et al.*, (1979) *Beyond Tea, Bingo and Condescension: The work of Task Force with Community Groups of Pensioners*

(Stoke on Trent: Beth Johnson Foundation in association with Task Force).

Bullock, A. (1960) *Life and Times of Ernest Bevin*, vol. 1 (London: Heinemann).

Burgess, E. W. (ed.) (1960) *Ageing in Western Societies* (University of Chicago Press).

Butcher, H. *et al.* (1980) *Community Groups in Action: Case studies and Analysis* (London: Routledge & Kegan Paul).

Butler, A. *et al.* (1979) *Sheltered Housing for the Elderly: A Critical Review* (Leeds University: Department of Social Policy and Administration).

Butler, D. B. and Stokes, D. (1971) *Political Change in Britain* (Harmondsworth: Penguin).

Butler, R. (1975) *Why Survive? Being Old in America* (New York: Harper & Row).

Butler, R. and Lewis, M. *Ageing and Mental Health* (St Louis: C. V. Mosby).

Carliner, L. (1969) 'Labour: The Anti-Youth Establishment', *New Generation*, vol. 11, pp. 27—31.

Carver, V. and Liddiard, P. (1978) *An Ageing Population: A Reader and Source Book* (London: Hodder & Stoughton in association with the Open University Press).

Carver, V. and Rodda, M. (1978) *Disability and the Environment* (London: Paul Elek).

Castle, B. (1980) *The Castle Diaries, 1974—6* (London: Weidenfeld & Nicolson).

Central Statistical Office (1981) *Social Trends*, No. 11 (London: HMSO).

Chebotarev, D. F. and Sachuk, N. N. (1980) 'Union of Soviet Socialist Republics', in Palmore, E. (ed.), *International Handbook on Ageing* (London: Macmillan).

Clough, D. 'All our Tomorrows', *Community Care*, 13 March 1980, pp. 29—30.

Cole, D. and Utting, J. (1962) *The Economic Circumstances of Old People* (Welwyn: Codicote Press).

Commission of the European Communities (1978) *The Attitude of the Working Population to Retirement* (Brussels: CEC).

Community Development Project (1977) *The Cost of Industrial Change* (London: CDP).

Confederation of Health Service Employees (1981) *In Defence of the Old* (London: COHSE).

Cooper, D. (1971) *The Death of the Family* (London: Allen Lane).

Corrigan, P. *et al.* (1978) *Socialist Construction and Marxist Theory* (London: Macmillan).

Counter Information Services (1980) *NHS: Condition Critical*, Anti-Report No. 26 (London: CIS).

Crawford, M. (1971) 'Retirement and Disengagement', *Human Relations*, vol. 24, pp. 255—78.

Crawford, M. (1972) 'Retirement and Role Playing', *Sociology*, vol. 6. pp. 217—36.

Crawford, M. (1973) 'Retirement: a rite de passage', *Sociological Review*, vol. 21, pp. 476—81.

Cypher, J. (1979) *Seebohm across Three Decades: Social Services Departments Past, Present and Future* (Birmingham: BASW Publications).

Davin, D. (1976) *Women—Work* (Oxford University Press).

Davis, N. (1976) 'Britain's Changing Age Structure': 1931—2011', *Population Trends*, Spring 1976, pp. 14—17.

Deacon, B. (1981) 'Social Administration, Social Policy and Socialism', *Critical Social Policy*, vol. 1, no. 1, pp. 43—66.

Delamont, S. (1981) *The Sociology of Women* (London: Allen & Unwin).

Department of Health and Social Security (1976) *Priorities for Health and Personal Social Services in England* (London: HMSO).

Department of Health and Social Security (1978) *A Happier Old Age* (London: HMSO).

Department of Health and Social Security (1980) *Inequalities in Health* (London: HMSO).

Department of Health and Social Security (1981) *Growing Older* (London: HMSO).

Doyal, L. (1979) *The Political Economy of Health* (London: Pluto Press).

Dumazedier, J. (1974) *Sociology of Leisure* (Amsterdam: Elsevier).

Dumbleton, B. and Shutt, J. (1979) 'Pensions: The Capitalist Trap', *New Statesman*, 7 September 1979, pp. 334—7.

Dunn, G. (no date) *The Story of the Federation* (Lancashire: NFOAPA).

Elder, G. (1977) *The Alienated: Growing Old Today* (London: Writers & Readers Publishing Co-operative).

Ensor, R. C. K. (1950) 'The Problems of Quality and Quantity in the British Population', *Eugenics Review*, vol. 13, no. 3, pp. 128—35.

Equal Opportunities Commission (1980) *The Experience of Caring for Elderly and Handicapped Dependants: Survey Report* (Manchester: EOC).

Erskine, A. and Phillipson, C. (1980) 'Self-Help, Education and Older People', in Glendenning, F. (ed.), *Outreach Education and the Elders: Theory and Practice* (Stoke on Trent: Beth Johnson Foundation).

Evers, H. (1981) 'Care or Custody? The Experience of Women Patients in Long-stay Geriatric Wards', in Hutter, B. and Williams, G. (eds), *Controlling Women: The Normal and the Deviant* (London: Croom Helm).

Fabian Society (1956) *Plan for Industrial Pensions (by a group of Trade Unionists)*, Fabian Tract No. 303 (London: Fabian Society).

Fairhurst, E. (1979) 'Experience of the Climacteric and the Ageing

176 REFERENCES

Woman', paper presented to the joint meeting of the British Society of Gerontology and British Geriatric Society for Research on Ageing (Glasgow).

Finch, J. and Groves, D. (1980). 'Community Care and the Family: A Case for Equal Opportunities', *Journal of Social Policy*, vol. 9., part 4, pp. 487–512.

Fischer, D. H. (1977) *Growing Old in America* (New York: Oxford University Press).

Fox, J. (1977) 'Effects of Retirement and Former Work Life on Women's Adaptation in Old Age', *Journal of Gerontology*, vol. 32, no. 2, pp. 196–202.

Fraser Brockington, C. (1965) *The Health of the Community*, 3rd edn (London: J. R. Churchill).

Friedmann, E. A. and Orbach, H. L. (1974) 'Adjustment to Retirement', in Arieti, S. (ed.), *American Handbook of Psychiatry*, vol. 1 (New York: Basic Books).

Fuld, H. and Robinson, K. V. (1953) 'Malnutrition in the Elderly', *The Lancet*, 24 October 1953.

Gamble, A. and Walton, P. (1976) *Capitalism in Crisis* (London: Macmillan).

Gardiner, J. (1981) 'Women, Recession and the Tories', *Marxism Today*, March 1981.

Gaudie, E. (1974) *Cruel Habitations: A History of Working Class Housing* (London: Allen & Unwin).

George, V. (1968) *Social Security: Beveridge and After* (London: Routledge & Kegan Paul).

Gilbert, B. B. (1970) *British Social Policy* (London: Batsford).

Gorz, A. (1974) *Socialism and Revolution* (London: Allen Lane).

Gough, I. (1979) *The Political Economy of the Welfare State* (London: Macmillan).

Government Actuary (1981) *Occupational Pension Schemes 1979: Sixth Survey* (London: HMSO).

Graebner, W. (1980) *A History of Retirement* (New Haven: Yale University Press).

Gray, B. and Isaacs, B. (1979) *Care of the Elderly Mentally Infirm* (London: Tavistock).

Gray, M. and Wilcock, G. (1981) *Our Elders* (Oxford University Press).

Gray Panthers (1976), 'Gray Panther History', mimeo (Philadelphia: Gray Panthers).

Guillemard, A. M. (1977) 'A Critical Analysis of Governmental Policies on Ageing from a Marxist Sociological Perspective: The Case of France, mimeo (Paris: Centre for the Study of Social Movements).

Guillemard, A. M. (1981) 'Old Age, Retirement, and the Social Class Structure', in Hareven, T. K. (ed.), *Dying and Life-Course Transitions* (New York: Guildford Press).

Harbridge, E. (1981) 'Very Sheltered Housing', *Community Care*, 24 July 1980, pp. 22–3.

Harris, A. (1968) *Social Welfare for the Elderly*, Government Social Survey (London: HMSO).

Harris, J. (1977) *William Beveridge: A Biography* (Oxford University Press).

Havighurst, R. J. *et al.* (eds), *Adjustment to Retirement* (Assen: Van Gorcum) (1969).

Heron, A. (1961) *Preparation for Retirement: Solving New Problems* (London: National Council of Social Services).

Hess, B. D. (ed) (1976) *Growing Old in America* (New Brunswick: Transaction Books).

Hessel, D. (1977) *Maggie Kuhn on Ageing* (London: Westminster Press).

Hewitt, P. (1974) *Age Concern on Pensioner Incomes* (London: Age Concern).

Heyman, D. K. and Jeffers, F. C. (1968) 'Wives and Husbands: A Pilot Study', *Journal of Gerontology*, vol. 23, pp. 488–96.

Hobman, D. (ed) (1978) *The Social Challenge of Ageing* (London: Croom Helm).

Hobson, D. (1978) 'Housewives: Isolation as Oppression', in *Women Take Issue: Aspects of Women's Subordination*, Women Studies Group (London: Hutchinson in association with CCCS, University of Birmingham).

Hobson, W. and Pemberton, J. (1955) *The Health of the Elderly at Home* (London: Butterworth).

Hochschild, A. R. (1978) *The Unexpected Community*, rev. edn (Berkeley: University of California Press).

Honigsbaum, F. (1979) *The Division in British Medicine* (London: Kogan Page).

Hubback, E. M. (1947) *The Population of Britain* (Harmondsworth: Penguin).

Hufton, O. H. (1974) *The Poor in Eighteenth Century France, 1750–1789* (Oxford University Press).

Hunt, A. (assisted by Fox, J.) (1970) *The Home Help Service in England and Wales*, Government Social Survey (London: HMSO).

Hunt, A. *The Elderly at Home*, OPCS Social Survey Division (London: HMSO).

Ingleby, D. (1976) 'Sanity, Madness and the Welfare State', in Wadsworth, M. and Robinson, D. (eds), *Studies in Everyday Medical Life* (London: Martin Robertson).

Isaacs, B. (ed.) 1978) *Recent Advances in Geriatric Medicine* (Edinburgh: Churchill).

Isaacs, B. (1980) 'Tough to be Old', in Dickson, N. (ed.), *Living in the 80s* (London: Age Concern).

Islington Task Force (1972) *Left in the Cold* (London: Task Force).

Jacobsohn, D. (1970) 'Attitudes towards Work and Retirement in Three Firms', Ph.D. thesis, London School of Economics.

Jacobsohn, D. (1972) 'The Influence of Fatigue-producing Factors in Industrial Work on Pre-retirement Attitudes', *Occupational Psychology*, vol. 46, pp. 193–200.

Jacobsohn, D. (1974) 'Rejection of the Retiree Role: A Study of Female Industrial Workers in the 50's', *Human Relations*, vol. 27, pp. 477–91.

Jones, C. *et al.* (forthcoming) 'Community Work and the Elderly', in Craig, G. *et al.*, *Radical Perspectives in Community Work* (London: Routledge & Kegan Paul).

Karn, V. (1977) *Retiring to the Seaside* (London: Routledge & Kegan Paul).

Kerckhoff, A. (1966) 'Husband–Wife Expectations and Reactions to Retirement', in Simpson J. H. and McKinney, J. C. (eds), *Social Aspects of Ageing* (Durham, North California: Duke University Press).

Kincaid, J. (1973) *Poverty and Equality in Britain* (Harmondsworth: Penguin).

Kinoy, S. K. (with the assistance of Heller, E.) (1979) 'Services to the Aged in the People's Republic of China' in Teicher, M. I. (ed.), *Reaching the Aged: Social Services in 44 Countries* (Beverly Hills: Sage).

Kirk, P. (1980) 'Owing to a Family Crisis', *New Society*, 17 January 1980.

Klass, A. (1975) *There's Gold in Them Thar Pills* (Harmondsworth: Penguin).

Knox, J. E. (1980) 'Prescribing for the Elderly in General Practice', Scottish General Practitioner Research Support Unit, *Journal of the Royal College of General Practitioners*, supplement no. 1, vol. 30.

Laslett, P. (1977) *Family Life and Illicit Love in Earlier Generations.* (Cambridge Univeristy Press).

Layard, R. *et al.* (1978) *The Causes of Poverty*, Royal Commission on the Distribution of Income and Wealth, Background Paper No. 5 (London: HMSO).

Lehr, U. and Dreher, G. (1969) 'Determinants of Attitudes towards Retirement', in Havighurst *et al.* (1969).

Lipman, A. (1961) 'Role Conceptions and Morale of Couples in Retirement', *Journal of Gerontology*, vol. 16, pp. 267–71.

Logan, W. P. D. (1953) 'Work and Age: Statistical Considerations', *British Medical Journal*, 28 November 1953, pp. 1190–3.

Long, P. (1979) 'Speaking out on Age', *Spare Rib*, no. 92, pp. 14–17.

Lopata, H. (1979) *Women as Widows* (Amsterdam: Elsevier).

Lunn, J. E. and Waters, W. H. R. (1969) 'A Study of Workload before and after Retirement at the Age of 65', *British Journal of Preventative and Social Medicine*, vol. 23, pp. 255—7.

Macfarlane, A. (1970) *Witchcraft in Tudor and Stuart England* (London: Routledge & Kegan Paul).

McGoldrick, A. and Cooper, C. (1980) 'Parting is not such Sorrow After All', *Financial Times*, 21 April 1980.

MacIntyre, S. (1977) 'Old Age as a Social Problem', in Dingwall, R. *et al.* (eds), *Health Care and Health Knowledge* (London: Croom Helm).

Malo, E. (1980) *The Politics of Housework* (London: Allison & Busby).

Marshall, V. (1981) 'Toleration of Ageing: Sociological Theory and Social Response to Population Ageing', *Proceedings of the IXth International Conference of Social Gerontology* (Paris: International Centre of Social Gerontology).

Means, R. (1981) *'Community Care' and Meals on Wheels* (Bristol: School for Advanced Urban Studies).

MIND (1979) *Mental Health of Elderly People* (London: MIND).

Ministry of Labour and National Service (1948—53) *Annual Reports* (for 1947, 1950 and 1952) (London: HMSO).

Ministry of Pensions and National Insurance (1966) *Financial and Other Circumstances of Retired Pensioners* (London: HMSO).

Minns, R. (1980) *Pensions Funds and British Capitalism* (London: Heinemann).

Minns, R. (1981) 'Challenging the Bankers', *New Statesman*, 21 August 1981, pp. 6—8.

Moroney, R. M. (1976) *The Family and the State* (London: Longman).

Munnichs, J. M. A. (1969) 'Role-patterns among Ageing and Aged Teachers and Steel-workers in the Netherlands', in Havighurst *et al.* (1969).

Myles, J. (1981) 'The Aged and the Welfare State: An Essay in Political Demography', paper to International Sociological Association Round Table, Old Age and Public Social Policies, Paris, 8—10 July 1981.

National Old People's Welfare Council (1952) *Report of the Sixth National Conference* (London: National Council of Social Services).

Neugarten, B. (1974) 'Age Groups in American Society and the Rise of the Young Old', *Annals of the American Academy of Political and Social Science*, vol. 415, pp. 187—98.

Newton, E. (1980) *This Bed My Centre* (London: Virago).

Nissel, M. (1980) 'The Family and the Welfare State', *New Society*, 7 August 1980.

Norman, A. J. (1980) *Rights and Risk* (London: Centre for Policy on Ageing).

Oakley, A. (1974) *Housewife* (London: Allen Lane).

OPCS (1979) *General Household Survey, 1977* (London: HMSO).

OPCS (1980) *Monitor*, May 1980.

Owen, A. D. K. (1935) 'Employees' Retirement Pension Schemes in Great Britain', *International Labour Review*, vol. 32, pp. 80–99.

Owen, F. (1979) 'The Health of the Old', *New Society*, 15 September 1977.

Palmore, E. (1973) 'Social Factors in Mental Illness', in Busse, E. W. and Pfeiffer, E. (eds), *Mental Illness in Later Life* (Washington: American Psychiatric Association).

Palmore, E. (1980) *International Handbook of Ageing* (London: Macmillan).

Parker, J. (1965) *Local Health and Welfare Services* (London: Allen & Unwin).

Parker, S. (1980) *Older Workers and Retirement*, OPCS Social Survey Division (London: HMSO).

Pelly, D. and Wise, V. (1980) *Trade Unions and Pension Funds* (London: CAITS, North-East London Polytechnic).

Peroni, F. (1981) 'The Status of Chronic Illness', *Social Policy and Administration*, vol. 15, no. 1, pp. 43–53.

Personal Social Services Council (1980) *Reductions in Local Authority Expenditure on the Personal Social Services* (London: PSSC).

Peters, A. and Weston, A. (1981) 'Cutting the Cake', *Spare Rib*, no. 104, pp. 39–41.

Piachaud, D. (1980) 'Social Security', in Bosanquet, N. and Townsend, P. (eds), *Labour and Equality: A Fabian Study of Labour in Power* (London: Heinemann).

Phillipson, C. (1977) *The Emergence of Retirement*, Working Papers in Sociology No. 14, Department of Sociology, University of Durham.

Phillipson, C. (1978) 'The Experience of Retirement: A Sociological Analysis', Ph.D. thesis, University of Durham.

Phillipson, C. (1980) 'The Politics of Ageing', *Bulletin on Social Policy*, no. 5, pp. 1–6.

Phillipson, C. (1981) 'Women in Later Life: Patterns of Control and Subordination', in Hutter, B. and Williams, G. (eds), *Controlling Women: The Normal and the Deviant* (London: Croom Helm).

Plank, D. (1978) 'Old People's Homes are not the Last Refuge', *Community Care*, 1 March 1978, pp. 16–18.

Political and Economic Planning (1948) *Population Policy in Great Britain* (London: PEP).

Pratt, H. J. (1974) 'Old Age Associations in National Politics', *Annals of the American Academy of Political and Social Science*, vol. 415, pp. 106–19.

Pratt, H. J. (1976) *The Gray Lobby* (University of Chicago Press).

Priestley, J. B. (1934) *English Journey* (London: Heinemann in association with Victor Gollancz, 1934; reprinted Harmondsworth: Penguin).

Puner, M. (1978) *To the Good Long Life* (London: Macmillan).

Putman, J. (1970) *Old Age Politics in California: From Richardson to Reagan* (California: Stanford University Press).

Pym, B. (1980) *Quartet in Autumn* (London: Granada).

Robb, B. (1967) *Sans Everything* (London: Nelson).

Rowbotham, S. (1973) *Women's Consciousness, Man's World* (Harmondsworth: Penguin).

Rowbotham, S. *et al.* (1980) *Beyond the Fragments: Feminism and the Making of Socialism* (London: Merlin Press).

Rowlings, C. (1981) *Social Work with Elderly People* (London: Allen & Unwin).

Rowntree, B. Seebohm (1947) *Old People: Report of a Survey Committee* (Oxford University Press).

Royal Commission on Population (1949) *Report* (London: HMSO).

Ryan, M. (1978) *The Organisation of Soviet Medical Care* (Oxford and London: Basil Blackwell and Martin Robertson).

Salaman, G. (1981) *Class and the Corporation* (London: Fontana).

Sennett, R. and Cobb, J. (1973) *The Hidden Injuries of Class* (New York: Vintage Books).

Sève, L. (1978) *Man in Marxist Theory and the Psychology of Personality* (Brighton: Harvester Press).

Shanas, E. *et al.* (eds) (1968) *Old People in Three Industrial Societies* (London: Routledge & Kegan Paul).

Sharpe, D. and Kay, M. (1977) 'Worrying Trends in Prescribing', *Modern Geriatrics*, vol. 7, no. 7, pp. 32–6.

Sheldon, J. H. (1948) *The Social Medicine of Old Age* (Oxford University Press).

Shenfield, B. E. (1957) *Social Policies for Old Age* (London: Routledge & Kegan Paul).

Shephard, R. J. (1978) *Physical Activity and Ageing* (London: Croom Helm).

Showler, B. and Sinfield, A. (1981) *The Workless State* (London: Martin Robertson).

Sinfield, A. (1968) *The Long-term Unemployed: A Comparative Survey* (Paris: OECD).

Skidelsky, R. (1970) *Politicians and the Slump* (Harmondsworth: Penguin).

Skidelsky, R. (1975) *Oswald Mosley* (London: Macmillan).

Smirnov, S. (1977) 'The Employment of Old-Age Pensioners in the USSR', *International Labour Review*, vol. 116, no. 1, pp. 87–94.

Stearns, P. (1975) *Lives of Labour* (London: Croom Helm).

Stearns, P. (1977) *Old Age in European Society: The Case of France* (London: Croom Helm).

Streib, G. F. and Schneider, S. J. (1971) *Retirement in American Society: Impact and Process* (Cornell University Press).

Stevenson, J. (1977) *Social Conditions in Britain Between the Wars* (Harmondsworth: Penguin).

Stott, M. (1973) *Forgetting's No Excuse* (London: Faber).

Taylor, I. *et al.* (1973) *The New Criminology* (London: Routledge & Kegan Paul).

Thane, P. (1978) 'The Muddled History of Retiring at 60 and 65', *New Society*, 3 August 1978, pp. 234–6.

Thomas, K. (1976) 'Age and Authority in Early Modern England', *Proceedings of the British Academy*, vol. LXII, pp. 205–48.

Thompson, E. P. (1967) 'Time, Work Discipline and Industrial Capitalism', *Past and Present*, no. 39, pp. 56–97.

Thompson, F. (1973) *Lark Rise Over Candleford* (London: Penguin).

Thompson, K. *et al.* (1952) *The Care of Old People*, Conservative Political Centre Discussion Series, Pamphlet No. 121 (London: CPC).

Thompson, P. (1975) *The Edwardians* (London: Weidenfeld & Nicolson).

Tinker, A. (1981) *The Elderly in Modern Society* (London: Longman).

Townsend, P. (1957) *The Family Life of Old People* (London: Routledge & Kegan Paul).

Townsend, P. (1962) *The Last Refuge* (London: Routledge & Kegan Paul).

Townsend, P. (1979) *Poverty in the United Kingdom* (Harmondsworth: Penguin).

Townsend, P. and Wedderburn, D. (1965) *The Aged in the Welfare State* (London: Bell).

Trade Union Studies Information Unit (1979) *Life Without Wages* (Newcastle: TUSIU).

Trades Union Congress (1928–9) *Reports on the Proceedings of the 60th and 61st Annual Congresses* (London: TUC).

Transport & General Workers' Union (1929) *Minutes of the Biennial Delegate Conference* (London: TGWU).

Treas, J. (1979) 'Socialist Organisation and Economic Development in China: Latent Consequences for the Aged', *The Gerontologist*, vol. 19, no. 1, pp. 34–43.

Victoria Residents' Association (1979) *First Annual Report* (Birmingham: VRA).

Walker, A. (1980) 'The Social Creation of Poverty and Dependency', *Journal of Social Policy*, vol. 9, no. 1, pp. 49–75.

Walker, A. (1981) 'Towards a Political Economy of Old Age', *Ageing and Society*, vol. 1, part 1, pp. 73–94.

Walker, K. (1952) *Commentary on Age* (London: Jonathan Cape).

Ward, S. (1981) 'Pension Scheme Trustees – Powers and Duties', *Labour Research*, October 1981, pp. 214–15.

Wedderburn, D. (1975) 'Prospects for the Re-organisation of Work', *The Gerontologist*, vol. 15, no. 3, pp. 236–41.

Wermal, M. T. and Gelbaum, S. (1945) 'Work and Retirement in Old Age', *American Journal of Sociology*, vol. 51, pp. 16–21.

Westergaard, J. and Resler, H. (1975) *Class in a Capitalist Society* (London: Heinemann).

Whitehouse, A. (1978) Interview with Maggie Kuhn, *New Age*, vol. 2, Winter 1978, pp. 7–9.

Wicks, M. (1978) *Old and Cold: Hypothermia and Social Policy* (London: Heinemann).

Willis, P. (1977) *Learning to Labour* (Farnborough: Saxon House).

Wilson, E. (1977) *Women and the Welfare State* (London: Tavistock).

Wilson, E. (1980) *Only Halfway to Paradise* (London: Tavistock).

Wilson, E. (1981) 'Socialist Welfare in the Eighties', in Bridges, G. and Brunt, R. (eds), *Silver Linings: Some Strategies for the Eighties*, (London: Lawrence & Wishart).

Wootton, B. (1959) *Social Sciences and Social Pathology* (London: Allen & Unwin).

Worsley, P. (1975) *Inside China* (London: Allen Lane).

Index

DATE DUE

DEMCO 38-297